SHAKESPEARE'S SONNETS
IN EASY READING VERSE

By the same author:

Shakespeare's Tragedies in Easy Reading Verse

Shakespeare's Comedies in Easy Reading Verse

Shakespeare's Histories & Romances in Easy Reading Verse

Chaucer's Canterbury Tales in Easy Reading Verse

Charles Dickens' Oliver Twist in Easy Reading Verse

Charles Dickens' A Christmas Carol in Easy Reading Verse

Kenneth Grahame's The Wind in the Willows in Easy Reading Verse

SHAKESPEARE'S SONNETS
in Easy Reading Verse

Richard Cuddington

Copyright © Richard Cuddington 2016
www.richardcuddington.co.uk

The right of Richard Cuddington to be identified as the author of this work has been asserted by him in accordance with the Copyright, Designs and Patents Act 1988.

This book is copyright material and must not be copied, reproduced, transferred or publicly performed or used in any way except as specifically permitted in writing by the author, as allowed under the terms and conditions under which it was produced or as strictly permitted by applicable copyright law. Any unauthorised distribution or use of this text may be a direct infringement of the author's rights.

First published in Great Britain by CompletelyNovel.com 2016

Cover design by Denis Grigorjuk

ISBN 9781849149501

Author's Note

These adaptations of William Shakespeare's Sonnets are not intended to be a line by line interpretation. Their purpose is to capture the overall substance and sentiment of each sonnet in easy to read, modern verse. In this way the author hopes that they will assist in the understanding of the original text, which follows each Easy Reading Verse adaptation.

1

From people who are beautiful
We desire a prize,
That they have children to ensure
Their beauty never dies.
And these sweet children left behind –
Fulfilling thus this duty,
Will forever bring to mind
The parent's unique beauty.
But you who are wrapped up in self
And in your own bright life,
Are spreading famine far and wide
And letting it run rife.
You starve the world of all you have –
Let love of self abound,
When truthfully you should now spread
Your beauty all around.
For you deny the world your genes
By being your own foe,
For you're the handsomest there is
As you must surely know.
You're beautiful like springtime,
Yet waste your beauty – why?
Because you should produce new life
Not let your beauty die.
Pity the world and share yourself,
Don't be a selfish knave,
Don't be the glutton who thus took
His beauty to the grave.

1

From fairest creatures we desire increase,
That thereby beauty's rose might never die,
But as the riper should by time decease,
His tender heir might bear his memory:
But thou, contracted to thine own bright eyes,
Feed'st thy light's flame with self-substantial fuel,
Making a famine where abundance lies,
Thyself thy foe, to thy sweet self too cruel:
Thou that art now the world's fresh ornament,
And only herald to the gaudy spring,
Within thine own bud buriest thy content,
And tender churl mak'st waste in niggarding:
Pity the world, or else this glutton be,
To eat the world's due, by the grave and thee.

2

When forty winters have passed by –
Carved trenches on your brow,
Diminishing the beauty that
You revel in right now,
And when that beauty's disappeared
Which nothing can disguise,
And you now have a wrinkled face
And deep, dark sunken eyes,
Why then if someone asked of you,
'Where has your beauty gone?'
And you replied, 'It is still here,
Where it has always shone.'
Why this would be a shameful act,
Such dastardly self praise,
Much better if you said your looks
Were lost by spending days,
In raising a delightful child,
Whose beauty did thus shine;
A child who would be constant there
To carry on your line,
And so the beauty of this child
That your good life has sown,
Would be the means to carry on
That beauty of your own.
For it's like being born again,
Made new when you are old,
With warm blood flowing through their veins
Although your own is cold.

2

When forty winters shall besiege thy brow,
And dig deep trenches in thy beauty's field,
Thy youth's proud livery so gazed on now,
Will be a tatter'd weed of small worth held:
Then being asked, where all thy beauty lies,
Where all the treasure of thy lusty days;
To say, within thine own deep sunken eyes,
Were an all-eating shame, and thriftless praise.
How much more praise deserv'd thy beauty's use,
If thou couldst answer 'This fair child of mine
Shall sum my count, and make my old excuse,'
Proving his beauty by succession thine!
This were to be new made when thou art old,
And see thy blood warm when thou feel'st it cold.

3

Look in the mirror, tell yourself
Now is the time that face,
Should have a child, it's truly due –
It is the time and place.
Your face is fresh and youthful now
But this will not last long,
And if you do not have a child
It surely would be wrong.
For you would cheat the world and then
Deny some worthy other,
To be your spouse and have the chance
To be a loving mother.
For do you think there's some so fair
Who would refuse you? – No.
Or are you so absorbed with self
That you don't wish to know
The joy of having children,
For it is rightly true,
Your mother sees her youthful days
When she looks now at you.
And when you're old you'll also see,
When gazing on your child,
A memory of long time past
When you were free and wild.
But if you choose to childless be
You'll die alone and rue,
The fact that when you leave this world
Your image dies with you.

3

Look in thy glass and tell the face thou viewest
Now is the time that face should form another;
Whose fresh repair if now thou not renewest,
Thou dost beguile the world, unbless some mother.
For where is she so fair whose unear'd womb
Disdains the tillage of thy husbandry?
Or who is he so fond will be the tomb,
Of his self-love to stop posterity?
Thou art thy mother's glass and she in thee
Calls back the lovely April of her prime;
So thou through windows of thine age shalt see,
Despite of wrinkles this thy golden time.
But if thou live, remember'd not to be,
Die single and thine image dies with thee.

4

You're wasting all your loveliness –
You spend it on yourself,
You store good Nature's legacy
Upon a selfish shelf.
Nature only lends us things
To share out as we live,
So why abuse this great largesse
That's given us to give?
We're granted gifts to spread about,
But living life alone,
Means you will leave no memory
Once all your years have flown.
By only thinking selfishly
You fool yourself for sure,
For you deny the best of you,
Deceive yourself and more.
For when fair Nature beckons you,
And calls you to be gone,
What mantle that's acceptable
Can you in truth then don?
The unused beauty that you had,
All fresh and once brand new,
Will surely have been wasted
And buried then with you.
But if you took the chance to use
That beauty now, you'd see
Your beauty would remain and thus
Preserve your memory.

4

Unthrifty loveliness, why dost thou spend
Upon thy self thy beauty's legacy?
Nature's bequest gives nothing, but doth lend,
And being frank she lends to those are free:
Then, beauteous niggard, why dost thou abuse
The bounteous largess given thee to give?
Profitless usurer, why dost thou use
So great a sum of sums, yet canst not live?
For having traffic with thy self alone,
Thou of thy self thy sweet self dost deceive:
Then how when nature calls thee to be gone,
What acceptable audit canst thou leave?
Thy unused beauty must be tombed with thee,
Which, used, lives th' executor to be.

5

The passing hours that gently worked
To frame that lovely gaze,
Upon the handsome face which has
The power to amaze
Will also be the instrument,
As time goes rushing by,
To play the tyrant and to cause
Your looks to slowly die.
And what is now so beautiful
Will quickly thus be gone,
For never resting time does lead
The summer quickly on
To hideous cold winter,
With all the land laid bare;
Sap checked with frost – leaves disappeared
And snow cast everywhere.
But summer is distilled for us,
Although now far away,
For we can hold the summer flowers
And make their perfume stay,
By saving summer in a glass,
With fragrance to abound –
Cast memories of summer days
By sweet smells all around.
For flowers distilled live on and thus
The winter's days do cheat,
For though their outward show is gone
Their fragrance smells still sweet.

5

Those hours, that with gentle work did frame
The lovely gaze where every eye doth dwell,
Will play the tyrants to the very same
And that unfair which fairly doth excel;
For never-resting time leads summer on
To hideous winter, and confounds him there;
Sap checked with frost, and lusty leaves quite gone,
Beauty o'er-snowed and bareness every where:
Then were not summer's distillation left,
A liquid prisoner pent in walls of glass,
Beauty's effect with beauty were bereft,
Nor it, nor no remembrance what it was:
But flowers distill'd, though they with winter meet,
Leese but their show; their substance still lives sweet.

6

And so don't let cold winter's hand
Destroy your summer beauty
Before it's taken and distilled,
For this then is your duty.
Preserve your beauty with a child
And truly be fulfilled,
For if you fail to procreate
It seems yourself you've killed.
And if you breed another you,
You'll very quickly see
What satisfying joy will come,
How happy you will be.
And if you have ten children,
Your beauty to uphold,
Well death would be as nothing,
Your joy will be tenfold.
Whatever could death do to you
If you should thus depart?
For you're safe in the knowledge and
So happy in your heart
That you'll live in your children,
And you can clearly see,
Your beauty's taken forward
Safe in posterity.
Don't be strong-willed and selfish,
For you are much too fair
To be a body – nothing more,
With just the worms for heir.

6

Then let not winter's ragged hand deface,
In thee thy summer, ere thou be distill'd:
Make sweet some vial; treasure thou some place
With beauty's treasure ere it be self-kill'd.
That use is not forbidden usury,
Which happies those that pay the willing loan;
That's for thy self to breed another thee,
Or ten times happier, be it ten for one;
Ten times thy self were happier than thou art,
If ten of thine ten times refigur'd thee:
Then what could death do if thou shouldst depart,
Leaving thee living in posterity?
Be not self-will'd, for thou art much too fair
To be death's conquest and make worms thine heir.

7

When in the east, that gracious light
Lifts up its burning head,
Why everyone pays homage as
Those warming rays are shed.
And all become absorbed and by
This new appearing sight,
The sacred majesty that is
The sun's bright, warming light.
And having climbed high in the sky,
Up to that heavenly hill,
The sun resembles a strong youth
And all adore him still.
The sun, it makes a pilgrimage,
Golden – 'cross the sky,
But gently now it starts to set
And sinks from up on high.
It's like an old, decrepit man,
Now feeble in its way,
All those that once looked on with awe
Now slowly turn away.
And this is not unlike you too,
For you should take a wife,
And then seek out to multiply
While in the noon of life.
For if you fail to act this way,
Before your youth is done,
You'll die alone without the joy
Of fathering a son.

7

Lo! in the orient when the gracious light
Lifts up his burning head, each under eye
Doth homage to his new-appearing sight,
Serving with looks his sacred majesty;
And having climb'd the steep-up heavenly hill,
Resembling strong youth in his middle age,
Yet mortal looks adore his beauty still,
Attending on his golden pilgrimage:
But when from highmost pitch, with weary car,
Like feeble age, he reeleth from the day,
The eyes, 'fore duteous, now converted are
From his low tract, and look another way:
So thou, thyself outgoing in thy noon:
Unlook'd, on diest unless thou get a son.

8

To hear sweet music should be good,
And it should make you glad,
For joy should thus delight in joy
And shouldn't make you sad.
So why do you like many things
That do not bring you joy,
And revel in those acts that have
The power to annoy?
If the sound of well tuned song
Does thus offend your ear,
It is because that music speaks
Of all you've come to fear.
It tells you of the proper part
That you should play in life,
By having children of your own
And with a loving wife.
See how the strings play thus in tune,
The one there with another,
Just like a father and a child,
Both with a happy mother.
They all as one, sing loud and clear,
As if from single throat,
A lovely tune in harmony,
One pleasing, single note.
It speaks a word of caution,
If you do not beware,
You'll stay a single person and
You'll have no child to care.

8

Music to hear, why hear'st thou music sadly?
Sweets with sweets war not, joy delights in joy:
Why lov'st thou that which thou receiv'st not gladly,
Or else receiv'st with pleasure thine annoy?
If the true concord of well-tuned sounds,
By unions married, do offend thine ear,
They do but sweetly chide thee, who confounds
In singleness the parts that thou shouldst bear.
Mark how one string, sweet husband to another,
Strikes each in each by mutual ordering;
Resembling sire and child and happy mother,
Who, all in one, one pleasing note do sing:
Whose speechless song being many, seeming one,
Sings this to thee: 'Thou single wilt prove none.'

9

Is it because you fear and dread
Your widow's tearful eye,
That you stay single, wary of
Her sorrow when you die?
But if you die and leave no child
The world will mourn for you,
Just like a grieving wife, the world
Will do what widows do.
'Twill mourn the fact you had no heir –
But if on your demise,
You left some kin, your widow then
Could see you in their eyes.
She'd see your long loved shape and form,
That image left behind,
By gazing on your children
She'd see you in her mind.
When people are unthrifty,
And spend their funds at will,
The money stays here in the world,
The world enjoys it still.
But if your beauty is not used,
And if you choose to sever
That beauty from the world – why then
Your beauty's lost forever.
No love towards the others here
Within his bosom sits
Who acts this way – and to himself
A shameful act commits.

9

Is it for fear to wet a widow's eye,
That thou consum'st thy self in single life?
Ah! if thou issueless shalt hap to die,
The world will wail thee like a makeless wife;
The world will be thy widow and still weep
That thou no form of thee hast left behind,
When every private widow well may keep
By children's eyes, her husband's shape in mind:
Look! what an unthrift in the world doth spend
Shifts but his place, for still the world enjoys it;
But beauty's waste hath in the world an end,
And kept unused the user so destroys it.
No love toward others in that bosom sits
That on himself such murd'rous shame commits.

10

Do not deny the shame of it,
For in the life you live,
You bear no love for anyone,
You have no love to give.
This much is clear and all can see
You also do not care
About yourself – and have no love
For others standing there.
But grant it's so, for it is true,
There's many that love you,
Yet you seem keen to wreck the roof
When you should make it new.
That I may change my mind, I ask
You give your thoughts a shove,
For should a hate be fairer lodged
Than kind and gentle love?
Be as your presence that all see,
The outward you they find,
Take care to show your better side,
Be gracious and be kind.
Or if you cannot manage this,
At least be kind of heart
Unto yourself, for this would be
At least a modest start.
Or have a child, if nothing more,
Than out of love of me,
Your beauty then would live through them,
For all of us to see.

10

For shame! deny that thou bear'st love to any,
Who for thy self art so unprovident.
Grant, if thou wilt, thou art belov'd of many,
But that thou none lov'st is most evident:
For thou art so possess'd with murderous hate,
That 'gainst thy self thou stick'st not to conspire,
Seeking that beauteous roof to ruinate
Which to repair should be thy chief desire.
O, change thy thought, that I may change my mind:
Shall hate be fairer lodg'd than gentle love?
Be, as thy presence is, gracious and kind,
Or to thyself at least kind-hearted prove:
Make thee another self for love of me,
That beauty still may live in thine or thee.

11

As fast as you shall wilt and grow
Feeble, meek and old,
You could again grow quickly as
Your children's lives unfold.
The fresh, young blood you would bestow
While you are still so young,
You could one day still claim your own
When sitting there among
Those children that are dear to you –
For in this very act,
They help to keep you light of heart,
And keep your youth intact.
In marriage and in children
Lies wisdom – beauty too,
And the knowledge that you've played
Your part to thus renew.
Without these precious, noble things,
Why it is true to say
Lies foolishness and dreary age
And creeping, cold decay.
If all were minded to this path,
There'd surely be a cost,
In three score years the human race
Would cease and so be lost.
Fair Nature's carved you out to thus
Procreate – thereby,
To print fair copies of yourself,
Not let your beauty die.

11

As fast as thou shalt wane, so fast thou grow'st,
In one of thine, from that which thou departest;
And that fresh blood which youngly thou bestow'st,
Thou mayst call thine when thou from youth convertest,
Herein lives wisdom, beauty, and increase;
Without this folly, age, and cold decay:
If all were minded so, the times should cease
And threescore year would make the world away.
Let those whom nature hath not made for store,
Harsh, featureless, and rude, barrenly perish:
Look, whom she best endow'd, she gave thee more;
Which bounteous gift thou shouldst in bounty cherish:
She carv'd thee for her seal, and meant thereby,
Thou shouldst print more, not let that copy die.

12

When I look at the clock that puts
The passing time to flight,
And see the last brave light of day
Turn into hideous night.
When I see glossy, flowing hair
Turning white with age,
And lofty trees bereft of leaves
At winter's early stage,
And summer crops stacked up in bales
That marks the summer's end,
Well then I think of you and what
All this might thus portend.
I think about your beauty,
And question – for I know
That you among the wastes of time
Will just as surely go.
For sweet and lovely people
Still see their beauty wane,
They die as fast as others grow,
Their beauty can't remain.
And nothing can give sound defence
Against the chilly clime
Created by the slicing scythe
Of ancient Father Time.
Except perhaps to procreate,
And so that you can say
That you've stood and defied time as
He carries you away.

12

When I do count the clock that tells the time,
And see the brave day sunk in hideous night;
When I behold the violet past prime,
And sable curls, all silvered o'er with white;
When lofty trees I see barren of leaves,
Which erst from heat did canopy the herd,
And summer's green all girded up in sheaves,
Borne on the bier with white and bristly beard,
Then of thy beauty do I question make,
That thou among the wastes of time must go,
Since sweets and beauties do themselves forsake
And die as fast as they see others grow;
And nothing 'gainst Time's scythe can make defence
Save breed, to brave him when he takes thee hence.

13

If you could always be yourself
How lovely that would be;
If you could live forever,
Be always there to see –
Why that would be just marvellous,
But as you'll die one day
You must pass on your beauty
In the usual way.
For that beauty's here on lease
And will come to an end,
So you should have some children soon,
So that you can then send
Your beauty to the future time,
So when the years fly by
You'll know your sweet form will remain
And it will never die.
For who would let a lovely house
Wither in decay,
When care would guard against gusts of
A stormy winter's day?
Or who would not take care to ease
The pain of growing old?
Take arms against the passing time
And death's eternal cold.
Only unthrifty souls would choose
To not make this their aim.
You had a father once my friend,
Your son should have the same.

13

O that you were your self; but, love you are
No longer yours, than you your self here live:
Against this coming end you should prepare,
And your sweet semblance to some other give:
So should that beauty which you hold in lease
Find no determination; then you were
Yourself again, after yourself's decease,
When your sweet issue your sweet form should bear.
Who lets so fair a house fall to decay,
Which husbandry in honour might uphold,
Against the stormy gusts of winter's day
And barren rage of death's eternal cold?
O, none but unthrifts. Dear my love, you know,
You had a father: let your son say so.

14

I do not see the stars above
And from them judgements pluck,
And yet I know astronomy –
But not to forecast luck.
I cannot foresee evil times
Or when a plague will strike,
Or tell with certainty just what
A season will be like.
Nor can I tell conclusively
What folk will lose or gain,
Or how a prince will fare – forecast
The thunder, wind and rain.
But I can see the future when
I look into your eyes;
They say that truth and beauty
Will together rise,
And you will live for evermore,
When your sweet life is done,
If you pass on yourself within
A daughter or a son.
And if you don't I do predict,
I think with accuracy,
A thing I feel is definite
That I can clearly see.
And that is when you die they'll say –
Because it is quite true –
On that doom ridden, mournful day
Your beauty died with you.

14

Not from the stars do I my judgement pluck;
And yet methinks I have astronomy,
But not to tell of good or evil luck,
Of plagues, of dearths, or seasons' quality;
Nor can I fortune to brief minutes tell,
Pointing to each his thunder, rain and wind,
Or say with princes if it shall go well
By oft predict that I in heaven find:
But from thine eyes my knowledge I derive,
And constant stars in them I read such art
As 'Truth and beauty shall together thrive,
If from thyself, to store thou wouldst convert';
Or else of thee this I prognosticate:
'Thy end is truth's and beauty's doom and date.'

15

When I consider all of life,
Everything that grows,
I very clearly see those things
That everybody knows.
For all that lives was perfect once –
Resplendent in its prime,
Enjoying moments in our world
But for the briefest time.
We live upon a vast, broad stage
Where our lives do entwine,
Influenced by stars above
As on our world they shine.
I see men grow as plants do too,
As time goes drifting by,
Cheered upon – then cruelly checked
Beneath the selfsame sky.
Youthful zest we celebrate,
When rising fresh and new,
It's just as quickly cut right down
And disappears from view.
When I think of life's fickleness,
You come into my sight,
And time debating with decay
To change your day to night.
And so I fight a war with time,
To keep you fresh and new,
To capture all you are in words
As time takes youth from you.

15

When I consider every thing that grows
Holds in perfection but a little moment,
That this huge stage presenteth nought but shows
Whereon the stars in secret influence comment;
When I perceive that men as plants increase,
Cheered and checked even by the self-same sky,
Vaunt in their youthful sap, at height decrease,
And wear their brave state out of memory;
Then the conceit of this inconstant stay
Sets you most rich in youth before my sight,
Where wasteful Time debateth with decay
To change your day of youth to sullied night,
And all in war with Time for love of you,
As he takes from you, I engraft you new.

16

But why not find a mightier way,
To go to war on time?
A better way to fight decay
Than by my worthless rhyme.
For these are now the happiest days
That you will ever see,
And many virtuous maidens would
Your fair wife like to be.
And they would have your children,
And through the passing hours,
Your children would become for you
Your lovely living flowers.
And they would form an image,
To be esteemed by men,
Above those from a painter's brush
Or from a poet's pen.
Time brought you to your present state
But cannot keep you there,
It can't preserve your inner worth
Or keep your outside fair.
And neither can my poetry,
But children will ensure,
That part of you goes on and on,
Preserved for evermore.
So give yourself away and then
You'll stay here ever still,
A part of you will thus remain,
Drawn by your own sweet skill.

16

But wherefore do not you a mightier way
Make war upon this bloody tyrant, Time?
And fortify your self in your decay
With means more blessed than my barren rhyme?
Now stand you on the top of happy hours,
And many maiden gardens, yet unset,
With virtuous wish would bear you living flowers,
Much liker than your painted counterfeit:
So should the lines of life that life repair,
Which this, Time's pencil, or my pupil pen,
Neither in inward worth nor outward fair,
Can make you live yourself in eyes of men.
To give away yourself, keeps yourself still,
And you must live, drawn by your own sweet skill.

17

Whoever will believe my verse
In future time to be,
If I extol you as you are
As I have come to see?
Although I must admit it's so
My words are like a tomb,
That hides your qualities as if
They're in a darkened room.
If I could write the words to show
The beauty of your eyes,
And all your grace – in future time
They'd say, 'This poet lies.
Such heavenly beauty never touched
A face upon this Earth.'
My poems would be scorned and said
To be of little worth.
And like old men who use their tongue,
But say no word that's true,
Whatever words were spoken
Would not give you their due,
And would be called a poet's whim –
That he had got it wrong,
Full of false words and rhetoric
As in an ancient song.
But if a child of yours should be
Alive in future time,
You would live twice – it must be said,
Through it and in my rhyme.

17

Who will believe my verse in time to come,
If it were fill'd with your most high deserts?
Though yet heaven knows it is but as a tomb
Which hides your life, and shows not half your parts.
If I could write the beauty of your eyes,
And in fresh numbers number all your graces,
The age to come would say 'This poet lies;
Such heavenly touches ne'er touch'd earthly faces.'
So should my papers, yellow'd with their age,
Be scorn'd, like old men of less truth than tongue,
And your true rights be term'd a poet's rage
And stretched metre of an antique song:
But were some child of yours alive that time,
You should live twice,--in it, and in my rhyme.

18

And so shall I compare you
To a summer's day?
For you are far more lovely
And temperate – in your way.
Rough winds, the buds of May do shake,
On gusty days they're caught,
And summer days go rushing by,
And summer seems too short.
Sometimes the sun – sweet heaven's eye –
May too strongly shine,
But sometimes clouds obscure its face
And beauty can decline.
In time all that is lovely,
Becomes a fleeting glance,
It disappears forever
By Nature's course or chance.
But your eternal summer
And beauty will not fade,
And death will never boast that you
Are wandering in the shade,
When you are caught, for all of time
In the entwining vines,
Of the heartfelt poetry,
Of my eternal lines.
So long as men have breath to breathe,
Or they have eyes to see,
My poem will live on and thus
It will give life to thee.

18

Shall I compare thee to a summer's day?
Thou art more lovely and more temperate:
Rough winds do shake the darling buds of May,
And summer's lease hath all too short a date:
Sometime too hot the eye of heaven shines,
And often is his gold complexion dimm'd,
And every fair from fair sometime declines,
By chance, or nature's changing course untrimm'd:
But thy eternal summer shall not fade,
Nor lose possession of that fair thou ow'st,
Nor shall death brag thou wander'st in his shade,
When in eternal lines to time thou grow'st,
So long as men can breathe, or eyes can see,
So long lives this, and this gives life to thee.

19

Devouring, all consuming Time –
Blunt the lion's paws;
Pluck the sharp, keen teeth right from
The fearsome tiger's jaws.
And make the wholesome earth devour
All creatures – in a flood,
And burn the long-lived phoenix
Within its own red blood.
And Time – make glad and sorry times,
As with swift feet you fly,
Do what you will with all delights
As days and years go by.
But there is one most heinous crime
That I will not allow,
Do not carve folds and wrinkles
Upon my love's fair brow.
Do not draw furrowed lines on him
With your old, antique pen,
Let him remain untainted as
A model for all men.
And Time, despite your efforts,
As you make way along,
My love will stay as handsome,
Despite your every wrong.
For what e'er you choose to do,
From bad to even worse,
My love will stay forever young
By living in my verse.

19

Devouring Time, blunt thou the lion's paws,
And make the earth devour her own sweet brood;
Pluck the keen teeth from the fierce tiger's jaws,
And burn the long-liv'd phoenix, in her blood;
Make glad and sorry seasons as thou fleets,
And do whate'er thou wilt, swift-footed Time,
To the wide world and all her fading sweets;
But I forbid thee one most heinous crime:
O, carve not with thy hours my love's fair brow,
Nor draw no lines there with thine antique pen;
Him in thy course untainted do allow
For beauty's pattern to succeeding men.
Yet, do thy worst old Time: despite thy wrong,
My love shall in my verse ever live young.

20

Your face is like a woman's,
Pretty as can be,
But you're a man, a master
As I can clearly see.
You have a woman's gentle heart,
But what is true of you –
You do not have a cheating way
As many women do.
Your eyes are bright and beautiful,
But do not roll around
In the way that women's rove,
As I have often found.
You gild all things you gaze upon,
A man who gains much praise,
And truthfully, you steal men's eyes,
And women's souls amaze.
To be a woman, you were made,
Then Nature changed her mind,
And added an appendage which
On only men you find.
And you would be entirely right,
If you would then deduce,
This addition is to me
Of totally no use.
So women can enjoy you,
And do it physically,
But I will keep your love and that
Will be enough for me.

20

A woman's face with nature's own hand painted,
Hast thou, the master mistress of my passion;
A woman's gentle heart, but not acquainted
With shifting change, as is false women's fashion:
An eye more bright than theirs, less false in rolling,
Gilding the object whereupon it gazeth;
A man in hue all 'hues' in his controlling,
Which steals men's eyes and women's souls amazeth.
And for a woman wert thou first created;
Till Nature, as she wrought thee, fell a-doting,
And by addition me of thee defeated,
By adding one thing to my purpose nothing.
But since she prick'd thee out for women's pleasure,
Mine be thy love and thy love's use their treasure.

21

It's not my style at all to write
Sycophantic verse,
To muse about a woman's face
And endlessly rehearse,
Extravagant, lush compliments,
Not when these ladies don
A false mask with their make up,
Which is just painted on.
Another poet writes this way,
For he does thus compare
Great beauty with the sun and moon
And all things that are rare,
With rich gems from the sea and earth –
With April's first-born flowers,
With everything so precious that
Adorns the passing hours.
But as I love and truly,
I only want to write
What I really see and know,
What's there before my sight.
Take any person in the world –
My love is just as fair,
But not as bright as all the stars
Fixed high in heaven's air.
Let them say more, who write brash verse,
I think it's flawed – uncouth,
For I'm not here to sell false praise,
I'm here to tell the truth.

21

So is it not with me as with that Muse,
Stirr'd by a painted beauty to his verse,
Who heaven itself for ornament doth use
And every fair with his fair doth rehearse,
Making a couplement of proud compare'
With sun and moon, with earth and sea's rich gems,
With April's first-born flowers, and all things rare,
That heaven's air in this huge rondure hems.
O, let me, true in love, but truly write,
And then believe me, my love is as fair
As any mother's child, though not so bright
As those gold candles fix'd in heaven's air:
Let them say more that like of hearsay well;
I will not praise that purpose not to sell.

22

My mirror will not make me think
That I am growing old,
If you're still looking young and lithe –
A beauty to behold.
But when I see Time's furrows
And wrinkles on your face,
I'll know that death is close at hand
And coming on apace.
For all your beauty on display
That I hold close and see,
Is like the raiments that I wear –
It's just as close to me.
And my own heart beats in your chest,
As also yours in mine,
So how can I be older then
If our lives so entwine?
And so my love be wary,
As I will also be,
For your heart lies within my breast
And my heart lies in thee.
And I will give protection to
Your heart in every way,
As a nurse would for a baby
On every single day.
But do not think I will return
Your heart if mine is slain,
You gave it to me readily,
Not to give back again.

22

My glass shall not persuade me I am old,
So long as youth and thou are of one date;
But when in thee time's furrows I behold,
Then look I death my days should expiate.
For all that beauty that doth cover thee,
Is but the seemly raiment of my heart,
Which in thy breast doth live, as thine in me:
How can I then be elder than thou art?
O, therefore love, be of thyself so wary
As I, not for myself, but for thee will;
Bearing thy heart, which I will keep so chary
As tender nurse her babe from faring ill.
Presume not on thy heart when mine is slain,
Thou gav'st me thine not to give back again.

23

Like an imperfect actor
Who hasn't learnt his part,
Or like a raging person
Who weakens his own heart
By exertion of a passion
Too strong for his own frame,
I too can't trust myself and thus
Will likely do the same.
For sometimes I forget to speak
What lovers all should say,
For when my love is strongest
I let it then decay.
I do not say the words I should,
I don't observe love's rite,
I do not tell my lover
Of all those things I might.
So let my poems speak for me
With much more eloquence
Than if I spoke – penned words can be
By way of recompense.
They'll plead my love, and better
Than my poor tongue can do,
Read in these silent, written words
The love I feel for you.
And when you read, you'll comprehend,
And it will too be seen,
Just how much I love you and
Exactly what I mean.

23

As an unperfect actor on the stage,
Who with his fear is put beside his part,
Or some fierce thing replete with too much rage,
Whose strength's abundance weakens his own heart;
So I, for fear of trust, forget to say
The perfect ceremony of love's rite,
And in mine own love's strength seem to decay,
O'ercharg'd with burthen of mine own love's might.
O, let my looks be then the eloquence
And dumb presagers of my speaking breast,
Who plead for love, and look for recompense,
More than that tongue that more hath more express'd.
O, learn to read what silent love hath writ:
To hear with eyes belongs to love's fine wit.

24

My eye has played the painter
And placed your beauty's form,
Deep within my heart and there
I'll keep your image warm.
My body is the frame that holds
This image to my heart,
And this perspective is the skill
That shows a painter's art.
To find the image of you there
I must just use my eyes,
And your eyes are the vehicle
To where my image lies.
What good turns our eyes perform,
What favours too they do,
My eyes have drawn your shape and form
And made me close to you.
And your eyes act as windows,
When all is said and done,
That let me look into my breast –
And then the lovely sun,
Delights to take a peep as well,
To see what it can see,
And its reward is then assured,
To gaze therein on thee.
Yet eyes can only do so much,
They lack a special art,
They can but draw just what they see,
They cannot know your heart.

24

Mine eye hath play'd the painter and hath stell'd,
Thy beauty's form in table of my heart;
My body is the frame wherein 'tis held,
And perspective it is best painter's art.
For through the painter must you see his skill,
To find where your true image pictur'd lies,
Which in my bosom's shop is hanging still,
That hath his windows glazed with thine eyes.
Now see what good turns eyes for eyes have done:
Mine eyes have drawn thy shape, and thine for me
Are windows to my breast, where-through the sun
Delights to peep, to gaze therein on thee;
Yet eyes this cunning want to grace their art,
They draw but what they see, know not the heart.

25

Let those in favour with their stars,
Who do adopt the ploy
Of boasting of their honours,
And all they do enjoy,
Who revel in their titles,
Of which they'll likely boast,
Just carry on – while I delight
In what I honour most.
It is your love that brings me joy,
Unlike the honoured rest,
It is your love that does confirm
That truly I am blessed.
Like favourites of great princes,
These honoured often are
Like marigolds in sunshine
Which nothing seems to mar.
And while they are thus shone upon
By the sun's warm eye,
All is well – but just one frown
Will make their glory die.
It's like a famous warrior
Who's finally defeated,
And has his honours stripped from him,
So cruelly mistreated.
Happy then am I to be
Loved – and so perceive
I'm where I cannot be removed,
And where I'll never leave.

25

Let those who are in favour with their stars
Of public honour and proud titles boast,
Whilst I, whom fortune of such triumph bars
Unlook'd for joy in that I honour most.
Great princes' favourites their fair leaves spread
But as the marigold at the sun's eye,
And in themselves their pride lies buried,
For at a frown they in their glory die.
The painful warrior famoused for fight,
After a thousand victories once foil'd,
Is from the book of honour razed quite,
And all the rest forgot for which he toil'd:
Then happy I, that love and am belov'd,
Where I may not remove nor be remov'd.

26

I am your servant, dearest love,
And to you strongly bound,
And I now write this note to you,
And not so I may sound
Like a most witty writer,
My note is more to show
That I adore you and you are
The loveliest I know.
I may seem wanting in my words
But hope I can impart,
A little of the love I feel
Deep here within my heart.
And this will give you some idea
Of what you mean to me,
And that in time you'll come to look
Upon me graciously.
And when my lucky star thus guides
My hand to write with skill,
To dress my tattered love to sound
Worthy – then I will
Boast to the world and everyone
How I do love you so;
I will not rest until I'm sure
That all around me know.
But till then I'll not reveal
My face – or let you see
My modest presence in your sight,
For you to challenge me.

26

Lord of my love, to whom in vassalage
Thy merit hath my duty strongly knit,
To thee I send this written embassage,
To witness duty, not to show my wit:
Duty so great, which wit so poor as mine
May make seem bare, in wanting words to show it,
But that I hope some good conceit of thine
In thy soul's thought, all naked, will bestow it:
Till whatsoever star that guides my moving,
Points on me graciously with fair aspect,
And puts apparel on my tatter'd loving,
To show me worthy of thy sweet respect:
Then may I dare to boast how I do love thee;
Till then, not show my head where thou mayst prove me.

27

Weary through from working hard
I hasten to my bed,
The favoured place when tired from toil –
But then thoughts fill my head,
As I go on a journey
Within my mind, I do
Much work through earnest thinking
Now my body's work is through.
It's then my thoughts, from far away,
In darkness come to thee,
I keep my eyelids open wide
And like a blind man see.
For though the world is very dark,
Your image is laid bare,
For as I lie within my bed,
With blackness everywhere,
I see you with my sightless view,
You're there within my sight,
And like a jewel just hanging in
That ghastly, black, old night,
You make that night look beautiful,
And so because of you,
I get no rest throughout the day,
And none at night time too.
For when the darkness gathers,
It's then I always find,
There is no comfort in my bed,
No quiet for my mind.

27

Weary with toil, I haste me to my bed,
The dear repose for limbs with travel tir'd;
But then begins a journey in my head
To work my mind, when body's work's expired:
For then my thoughts--from far where I abide--
Intend a zealous pilgrimage to thee,
And keep my drooping eyelids open wide,
Looking on darkness which the blind do see:
Save that my soul's imaginary sight
Presents thy shadow to my sightless view,
Which, like a jewel (hung in ghastly night,
Makes black night beauteous, and her old face new.
Lo! thus, by day my limbs, by night my mind,
For thee, and for myself, no quiet find.

28

So how can I be happy
And feel that I am blessed,
When I am barred from gaining
The benefit of rest?
The oppression felt in day time
Is not relieved at night,
So day by night and night by day,
Oppression I do fight.
Though day and night are enemies,
They've shaken hands to be
My foes and thus together,
Conspire to torture me.
The daytime tortures me with toil,
And then the whole night through,
I'm tortured with the thoughts of how
I am so far from you.
I tell the day to please him,
How very bright you are,
So bright you take the place of sun,
When clouds, the day does mar.
I use you too to flatter
The black complexioned night,
To say how you light up the sky
When stars don't shine so bright.
Each weary day does daily make
My sorrows even longer,
And night by night my grief becomes
Prolonged and even stronger.

28

How can I then return in happy plight,
That am debarr'd the benefit of rest?
When day's oppression is not eas'd by night,
But day by night and night by day oppress'd,
And each, though enemies to either's reign,
Do in consent shake hands to torture me,
The one by toil, the other to complain
How far I toil, still farther off from thee.
I tell the day, to please him thou art bright,
And dost him grace when clouds do blot the heaven:
So flatter I the swart-complexion'd night,
When sparkling stars twire not thou gild'st the even.
But day doth daily draw my sorrows longer,
And night doth nightly make grief's length seem stronger.

29

When in disgrace with everyone,
Reviled in all men's eyes,
And when I trouble heaven
With futile, unheard cries.
And when I sit alone – bemoan,
About my outcast state,
And look upon my sorry self
And curse and rue my fate,
That's when I wish that I could have
More hope to help me through,
And also that I too possessed,
Good friends both strong and true.
I wish I had the attributes
Of that man over there,
I wish that life was kinder and
Was not quite so unfair.
And so I get myself into
A state of self despising,
Then think of you and soon my mood
Is like a lark a-rising,
From sullen earth into the sky
At the break of day,
And thoughts of you just lift me up
In such a love filled way.
And your sweet love remembered,
With all the joy it brings,
Is something I would not exchange
For all the wealth of kings.

29

When in disgrace with fortune and men's eyes
I all alone beweep my outcast state,
And trouble deaf heaven with my bootless cries,
And look upon myself, and curse my fate,
Wishing me like to one more rich in hope,
Featur'd like him, like him with friends possess'd,
Desiring this man's art, and that man's scope,
With what I most enjoy contented least;
Yet in these thoughts my self almost despising,
Haply I think on thee,-- and then my state,
Like to the lark at break of day arising
From sullen earth, sings hymns at heaven's gate;
For thy sweet love remember'd such wealth brings
That then I scorn to change my state with kings.

30

When on my own I sit awhile
And summon up the past,
The memories of all things gone –
And then I do contrast
Remembrance of those once lived times
With the depressing thought,
How I now lack and do not have
So many things I sought.
And with regret I cry new tears
From eyes that seldom flow.
I weep for precious friends who've died
That I once used to know.
I cry for loves who've long since gone
And moan through day and night,
Of many things I valued once
Now vanished from my sight.
I grieve of grievances I thought
That I'd let go and slain,
That I had left behind but now
They all come back again.
I feel the pain within my frame,
I feel it all once more,
As if I'd not paid for this hurt,
Not settled it before.
But if a while I think of you,
My very close dear friend,
Why all my losses are restored,
And all my sorrows end.

30

When to the sessions of sweet silent thought
I summon up remembrance of things past,
I sigh the lack of many a thing I sought,
And with old woes new wail my dear time's waste:
Then can I drown an eye, unused to flow,
For precious friends hid in death's dateless night,
And weep afresh love's long since cancell'd woe,
And moan the expense of many a vanish'd sight:
Then can I grieve at grievances foregone,
And heavily from woe to woe tell o'er
The sad account of fore-bemoaned moan,
Which I new pay as if not paid before.
But if the while I think on thee, dear friend,
All losses are restor'd and sorrows end.

31

You are endeared by all the hearts
Of those – it must be said,
Who once loved me, but through neglect
I have supposed them dead.
Within your heart, why there reigns love
And all its tender ways,
Along with all those friends I thought
Now buried for long days.
How many a tear of mourning love
Has fallen from my eye,
But now it does appear these loves
Hidden in you lie.
They're held by you – and closely too,
And have become a part
Of everything you are and now
They're held within your heart.
You're like a grave where buried love
Continues thus to live,
You own the love that once before
I owed to them to give.
And now that love I owed to them,
From me and me alone,
Is now your love and yours to have
And so to freely own.
And I see everyone I've loved
Or been loved by, in thee,
And as you have them all you now
Have all of all of me.

31

Thy bosom is endeared with all hearts,
Which I by lacking have supposed dead;
And there reigns Love, and all Love's loving parts,
And all those friends which I thought buried.
How many a holy and obsequious tear
Hath dear religious love stol'n from mine eye,
As interest of the dead, which now appear
But things remov'd that hidden in thee lie!
Thou art the grave where buried love doth live,
Hung with the trophies of my lovers gone,
Who all their parts of me to thee did give,
That due of many now is thine alone:
Their images I lov'd, I view in thee,
And thou--all they--hast all the all of me.

32

If you survive me, living on
When fickle death does cover
My dusty bones – and then you read
The words of me, your lover:
And reading this, the poor, crude lines,
Of he who loved you true,
Do not compare them with the words
Of verse that's fresh and new.
For men then will be better
At writing clever rhyme,
Much better than the men like me
Who write in this our time.
And though I will have been surpassed
By skilled and smarter men,
Keep my poems for my love,
Not power of my pen.
And keep in mind the kindly thought,
'If my friend's skill had grown,
With the advantage of this age,
His pen would then have sown
Poems of such beauty for
The love he felt inside,
Would have given birth to verse,
Proclaimed both far and wide.
But since he's dead and poets now
With him – are ranked above,
I'll read their poems for their skill
And I'll read his for love.'

32

If thou survive my well-contented day,
When that churl Death my bones with dust shall cover
And shalt by fortune once more re-survey
These poor rude lines of thy deceased lover,
Compare them with the bett'ring of the time,
And though they be outstripp'd by every pen,
Reserve them for my love, not for their rhyme,
Exceeded by the height of happier men.
O, then vouchsafe me but this loving thought:
'Had my friend's Muse grown with this growing age,
A dearer birth than this his love had brought,
To march in ranks of better equipage:
But since he died and poets better prove,
Theirs for their style I'll read, his for his love'.

33

I've seen many glorious mornings
When high up in the sky,
I've watched the warming, golden rays
Of the sun's bright eye.
It causes mountain tops to glow,
It kisses meadows green,
It gilds the bubbling streams that flow
With blithe and sparkling sheen.
But then the sun allows dark clouds
To show another side,
They come and make the world forlorn,
Its lovely light to hide.
And so the sun then disappears,
It hides its lovely face,
Stealing unseen into the west,
In sorry, lost disgrace.
And just like this, one early morn
The splendid sun did shine,
He shone upon my brow – but then
For but an hour was mine.
The clouds then masked the sun from view,
'Twas gone without a trace,
But I don't hold a grudge although
I lost his smiling face.
For men can act the selfsame way
When all is said and done,
For they can shame themselves just like
The heavenly, warm sun.

33

Full many a glorious morning have I seen
Flatter the mountain tops with sovereign eye,
Kissing with golden face the meadows green,
Gilding pale streams with heavenly alchemy;
Anon permit the basest clouds to ride
With ugly rack on his celestial face,
And from the forlorn world his visage hide,
Stealing unseen to west with this disgrace:
Even so my sun one early morn did shine,
With all triumphant splendour on my brow;
But out! alack! he was but one hour mine,
The region cloud hath mask'd him from me now.
Yet him for this my love no whit disdaineth;
Suns of the world may stain when heaven's sun staineth.

34

Why did you make a promise, sun?
That I could make my way,
And travel forth without my cloak
On a most beauteous day,
Only for me to quickly find
That I would need my cloak,
As clouds obscured you, lovely sun,
Like mist or fog or smoke.
And it is not enough to see
Your face break through the cloud,
To dry the rain upon my face
And leave me quite unbowed.
For though it maybe cures the wound
On my storm-beaten face,
It does not cure the slight I feel
Or lessen the disgrace.
And though you do repent your act,
Yet still I feel the loss,
For though you're sorry I still bear
The strong offence's cross.
When somebody thus takes from you –
Their sorrow's scant relief;
You still feel the invasion and
The victim of a thief.
But still the tears you shed for me
Are pearls and aid my needs,
For they all make amends and for
Your thoughtless, selfish deeds.

34

Why didst thou promise such a beauteous day,
And make me travel forth without my cloak,
To let base clouds o'ertake me in my way,
Hiding thy bravery in their rotten smoke?
'Tis not enough that through the cloud thou break,
To dry the rain on my storm-beaten face,
For no man well of such a salve can speak,
That heals the wound, and cures not the disgrace:
Nor can thy shame give physic to my grief;
Though thou repent, yet I have still the loss:
The offender's sorrow lends but weak relief
To him that bears the strong offence's cross.
Ah! but those tears are pearl which thy love sheds,
And they are rich and ransom all ill deeds.

35

Do not be grieved by what you did,
For this I can abide,
For everything within the world
Has an imperfect side.
For roses have their thorns that prick
And fountains have their mud,
And loathsome insects live within
The sweetest flower's bud.
And eclipses hide the moon
And cover up the sun,
And clouds, they do the same as well,
Bring gloom on everyone.
All men do things that are not right,
Even me as well.
As I forgive your faults I then
Corrupt myself and tell,
Excuses for your sensual deeds,
The things that you do wrong,
Even though they're little sins
And have been all along.
And so the person injured by
Your actions through and through,
Is now here acting in defence
And standing up for you.
I'm so confused 'twixt love and hate,
Conflicted I would say,
That I can't help but aid the thief
Who robs from me each day.

35

No more be griev'd at that which thou hast done:
Roses have thorns, and silver fountains mud:
Clouds and eclipses stain both moon and sun,
And loathsome canker lives in sweetest bud.
All men make faults, and even I in this,
Authorizing thy trespass with compare,
Myself corrupting, salving thy amiss,
Excusing thy sins more than thy sins are;
For to thy sensual fault I bring in sense,--
Thy adverse party is thy advocate,--
And 'gainst myself a lawful plea commence:
Such civil war is in my love and hate,
That I an accessary needs must be,
To that sweet thief which sourly robs from me.

36

I freely do accept the fact
That though you own my heart,
Despite the fact we are in love,
The two of us must part.
For blots on reputation
For which we've been berated,
And which together we incurred
And both of us created,
Can then be taken by myself
And borne by me alone,
Without your help, I'll take all fault
And bear it on my own.
Although our love is stronger still,
We're in this dreadful plight,
And though in love, it steals from us
Sweet hours of love's delight.
For I must not acknowledge you,
As this would bring you shame,
And you can't honour me – this would
Take honour from your name.
So never give me favour
Or public kindness show,
For it is better if it seems
That you don't wish to know.
But I love you so very much –
And as I think I've shown,
Your reputation's dear to me
As if it were my own.

36

Let me confess that we two must be twain,
Although our undivided loves are one:
So shall those blots that do with me remain,
Without thy help, by me be borne alone.
In our two loves there is but one respect,
Though in our lives a separable spite,
Which though it alter not love's sole effect,
Yet doth it steal sweet hours from love's delight.
I may not evermore acknowledge thee,
Lest my bewailed guilt should do thee shame,
Nor thou with public kindness honour me,
Unless thou take that honour from thy name:
But do not so, I love thee in such sort,
As thou being mine, mine is thy good report.

37

As a decrepit father
Takes pleasure in the sight
Of his child's youthful, active deeds,
That fill him with delight,
So I, by fortune's spite, made weak
Take comfort in your worth,
I see how truthfulness in you
Has thus been given birth.
For whether beauty, wealth or wit
Are held within your store,
Or some of those great attributes,
Or maybe even more,
What e'er the case, I'll graft my love
To them – for I believe
That loving them will surely help
My weakness to relieve.
For I'll no longer be despised,
Borne down, reviled and poor,
And this belief of mine will then
Sustain me evermore.
And I rejoice that you're so blessed,
And through your lucky story,
I can then be a part of all
Your glowing, warming glory.
I want the very best for you,
That's what I wish to see,
And since I have this earnest wish,
I'll ten times lucky be.

37

As a decrepit father takes delight
To see his active child do deeds of youth,
So I, made lame by Fortune's dearest spite,
Take all my comfort of thy worth and truth;
For whether beauty, birth, or wealth, or wit,
Or any of these all, or all, or more,
Entitled in thy parts, do crowned sit,
I make my love engrafted, to this store:
So then I am not lame, poor, nor despis'd,
Whilst that this shadow doth such substance give
That I in thy abundance am suffic'd,
And by a part of all thy glory live.
Look what is best, that best I wish in thee:
This wish I have; then ten times happy me!

38

How can I lack the wit to write
While you are here alive?
For you breathe life into my verse,
I have no need to strive.
You give me inspiration
Because you truly are
The sweetest person in the world,
A bright and shining star.
And as you are so wonderful,
There really is no doubt,
You are too fair for common scribes
To ever write about.
And if you see within my words
That come into your view,
Anything that's worthy – please
Give credit all to you.
And who could fail to write, indeed
When seeing such a sight,
For your fair beauty – this alone
Will great invention light.
And he that looks to be inspired
By gazing at your form,
Why let him pen eternal verse
That's way above the norm.
And if my words give pleasure to
The folk of current days,
Let pain of writing all be mine,
But you shall have the praise.

38

How can my muse want subject to invent,
While thou dost breathe, that pour'st into my verse
Thine own sweet argument, too excellent
For every vulgar paper to rehearse?
O, give thy self the thanks, if aught in me
Worthy perusal stand against thy sight;
For who's so dumb that cannot write to thee,
When thou thy self dost give invention light?
Be thou the tenth Muse, ten times more in worth
Than those old nine which rhymers invocate;
And he that calls on thee, let him bring forth
Eternal numbers to outlive long date.
If my slight muse do please these curious days,
The pain be mine, but thine shall be the praise.

39

How can I write about your worth
When you're a part of me?
Indeed it's true, the better part
As all can clearly see.
But when I praise you it will seem
Conceited – for it's true,
I praise my own unworthy self
When I lay praise on you.
And so dear love, let's be apart,
Let us divided live,
So that the praise that you deserve
I can still freely give.
And in this way, our dear, sweet love
Will lose its single name,
And by this separation
Your worth I can proclaim.
Your absence would be torment,
Except that it would leave
Time to dwell on thoughts of love
And thus no time to grieve.
The hours would pass by sweetly
And it would be sublime,
To think of you and all you are
To fill the passing time.
So I'll divide my love in two,
It will become a pair,
True love will stay here in my heart,
While you remain elsewhere.

39

O, how thy worth with manners may I sing,
When thou art all the better part of me?
What can mine own praise to mine own self bring?
And what is't but mine own when I praise thee?
Even for this, let us divided live,
And our dear love lose name of single one,
That by this separation I may give
That due to thee which thou deserv'st alone.
O absence! what a torment wouldst thou prove,
Were it not thy sour leisure gave sweet leave,
To entertain the time with thoughts of love,
Which time and thoughts so sweetly doth deceive,
And that thou teachest how to make one twain,
By praising him here who doth hence remain.

40

Take all my loves from me, my dear,
I say, yes, take them all,
Take every love I cherish,
All loves both large and small.
And when this is completely done
And you cannot do more,
What have you gained I humbly ask
That wasn't yours before?
For you already had my love,
You had my very best,
What was mine to give you had
Before you took the rest.
And as you take this love you should
Be prepared to be
My sweet lover – as you're theirs –
Make tender love with me.
But I forgive your robbery,
Oh sweet and gentle thief,
Although you take and do not give
And it does cause me grief.
For every lover is aware
And does so surely know,
A wrong done from a lover is
Much worse than from a foe.
And so my love – even if
You kill me, cause me woes,
I will remain a loyal friend,
For we must not be foes.

40

Take all my loves, my love, yea take them all;
What hast thou then more than thou hadst before?
No love, my love, that thou mayst true love call;
All mine was thine, before thou hadst this more.
Then, if for my love, thou my love receivest,
I cannot blame thee, for my love thou usest;
But yet be blam'd, if thou thy self deceivest
By wilful taste of what thyself refusest.
I do forgive thy robbery, gentle thief,
Although thou steal thee all my poverty:
And yet, love knows it is a greater grief
To bear love's wrong, than hate's known injury.
Lascivious grace, in whom all ill well shows,
Kill me with spites yet we must not be foes.

41

Those little wrongs that you commit
When we are far apart,
Those liberties you take when I
Am absent from your heart,
Are understandable – for you
Are handsome and it's so,
You're victim to temptation
Where e'er you choose to go.
For women do pursue you,
And when a woman woos,
What man, this opportunity
Would ever choose to lose?
But you should curb your straying youth,
And kind sir, forebear
From flirting with that lady
For whom I greatly care.
She is the love of this my life,
I beg you leave her be,
For she's my lady and my love
And she belongs to me.
So your libido, you must quell,
It's leading you astray,
And leave my mistress all alone
Those days when I'm away.
For your beauty is temptation,
It draws her thus to thee,
And your beauty is the reason
That makes you false to me.

41

Those pretty wrongs that liberty commits,
When I am sometime absent from thy heart,
Thy beauty, and thy years full well befits,
For still temptation follows where thou art.
Gentle thou art, and therefore to be won,
Beauteous thou art, therefore to be assail'd;
And when a woman woos, what woman's son
Will sourly leave her till he have prevail'd?
Ay me! but yet thou might'st my seat forbear,
And chide thy beauty and thy straying youth,
Who lead thee in their riot even there
Where thou art forced to break a twofold truth:--
Hers by thy beauty tempting her to thee,
Thine by thy beauty being false to me.

42

That you now have my former love
Is not my only pain,
And yet it must be clearly said
Time and time again,
That I once loved her dearly but
What really makes me cry
Is that she has you now – not me,
And yes – I wonder why?
But you two lovers who offend,
How do I thus exert
A rationale to ease my pain
And to relieve the hurt?
Well my friend – you love her so –
Because you know I do,
And she allows your constant praise
Because she knows that you
Are my close friend – and if I lose
Your friendship – and incur
A coolness thus between us,
Then it's a gain for her.
If I lose her – you win, for then
You find what I have lost,
And when you find each other,
I lose both and to my cost.
But here's the joy – my friend and I
Are one – and so you see,
My love is mine and totally
For she loves only me.

42

That thou hast her it is not all my grief,
And yet it may be said I loved her dearly;
That she hath thee is of my wailing chief,
A loss in love that touches me more nearly.
Loving offenders thus I will excuse ye:
Thou dost love her, because thou know'st I love her;
And for my sake even so doth she abuse me,
Suffering my friend for my sake to approve her.
If I lose thee, my loss is my love's gain,
And losing her, my friend hath found that loss;
Both find each other, and I lose both twain,
And both for my sake lay on me this cross:
But here's the joy; my friend and I are one;
Sweet flattery! then she loves but me alone.

43

My eyes see best when I'm asleep,
And this is unexpected,
But it is just because all day
They view things disrespected.
But when I sleep I dream of you,
My eyes shine oh so bright,
They lighten up your image in
The blackness of the night.
And as your shadow in the dark
Illumes my dreams, I know
That in the clearness of the day
How bright your light would glow.
But then what good is this to me,
To see you in the day,
When in the very dead of night
Your image does display.
It falls upon my sightless eyes
And in my mind I keep,
A perfect picture of your form
While heavily asleep.
And every day that passes
Is like the night to me,
Until the opportunity
To once again see thee.
And every night is bright as day,
Least that's the way it seems,
For when I'm sleeping in the dark
I see you in my dreams.

43

When most I wink, then do mine eyes best see,
For all the day they view things unrespected;
But when I sleep, in dreams they look on thee,
And darkly bright, are bright in dark directed.
Then thou, whose shadow shadows doth make bright,
How would thy shadow's form form happy show
To the clear day with thy much clearer light,
When to unseeing eyes thy shade shines so!
How would, I say, mine eyes be blessed made
By looking on thee in the living day,
When in dead night thy fair imperfect shade
Through heavy sleep on sightless eyes doth stay!
 All days are nights to see till I see thee,
 And nights bright days when dreams do show thee me.

44

If I were formed by thought and not
Dull flesh – it would be true,
A great and painful distance
Would not keep me from you.
For then despite the time and space –
And how so ever far –
From the remotest place of all,
I'd come to where you are.
And it would be of no account
That my poor foot did stand
At the farthest point from you,
For thought can jump 'cross land,
And nimbly too it can then leap
Across the seething sea,
For thought can visualise the place
Whereon it wants to be.
But the thought that kills me most
Is that I am not thought,
So when you're gone I cannot leap
The miles and cut them short.
Instead, I'm made of water
And earth – my body groans,
As I attempt to pass the time
With heartfelt, heavy moans.
And the elements that make me
Give nothing else to show,
But heavy, wet and woeful tears
As endlessly they flow.

44

If the dull substance of my flesh were thought,
Injurious distance should not stop my way;
For then despite of space I would be brought,
From limits far remote, where thou dost stay.
No matter then although my foot did stand
Upon the farthest earth remov'd from thee;
For nimble thought can jump both sea and land,
As soon as think the place where he would be.
But, ah! thought kills me that I am not thought,
To leap large lengths of miles when thou art gone,
But that so much of earth and water wrought,
I must attend time's leisure with my moan;
Receiving nought by elements so slow
But heavy tears, badges of either's woe.

45

There are two other elements,
Slight air and purging fire,
The first, the air, is all my thoughts,
The other my desire.
And both of them are with you,
Wherever I may be,
For they slide in swift motion
Between you dear and me.
And as I am four elements,
Earth, water, fire and air,
When air and fire go off to you,
I sink into despair.
I'm oppressed with melancholy
And aching for new breath,
When air and fire are absent,
I feel I'm close to death.
But then when they return from you
I am relieved of pain,
And once again I am restored
And feel myself again.
And now they're back I am assured,
And do believe it's true,
That you are in good health and that
The world is well with you.
I'm joyful – then I quickly feel
Distraught, no longer glad,
And so I send them back again
And straightaway feel sad.

45

The other two, slight air, and purging fire
Are both with thee, wherever I abide;
The first my thought, the other my desire,
These present-absent with swift motion slide.
For when these quicker elements are gone
In tender embassy of love to thee,
My life, being made of four, with two alone
Sinks down to death, oppress'd with melancholy;
Until life's composition be recur'd
By those swift messengers return'd from thee,
Who even but now come back again, assur'd,
Of thy fair health, recounting it to me:
This told, I joy; but then no longer glad,
I send them back again, and straight grow sad.

46

My eyes, my heart are both at war,
They're fighting one another,
They're both at mortal loggerheads,
The one there with the other.
They're fighting over who's in charge
Of your sweet image – for
The both of them claim ownership,
And that's why they're at war.
My heart does plead your image is
In him and not my eyes –
But then my eyes insist, in them,
Is where your image lies.
And so they argue back and forth,
So I must throw a light
Upon this disagreement and
Decide which one is right.
So I have formed a little team,
To take all this apart,
Made of my thoughts – who all pay thus
Deference to my heart.
So they've been set a puzzle
As if it were a quiz,
And now they've formed a verdict,
And so then – here it is.
My eyes are granted solely
Rights to your outward part,
The right to love you and be loved,
Why that goes to my heart.

46

Mine eye and heart are at a mortal war,
How to divide the conquest of thy sight;
Mine eye my heart thy picture's sight would bar,
My heart mine eye the freedom of that right.
My heart doth plead that thou in him dost lie,--
A closet never pierc'd with crystal eyes--
But the defendant doth that plea deny,
And says in him thy fair appearance lies.
To side this title is impannelled
A quest of thoughts, all tenants to the heart;
And by their verdict is determined
The clear eye's moiety, and the dear heart's part:
As thus; mine eye's due is thy outward part,
And my heart's right, thy inward love of heart.

47

And now my eye and heart have called
A truce – they have made friends,
Each does the other kindnesses,
They seek the selfsame ends.
And when my eye is famished,
For just one look at you,
And when my heart is smothered,
With sighs of love there too,
Why then my eye does feast upon
A picture of my love,
And bids my heart to look as well,
Upon my turtledove.
And then again another time,
My eye is my heart's guest,
And then my heart shares thoughts of love
With which he has been blessed.
And so my love, it's truly so
That you are always near,
Through your picture or my love,
Your presence is still here.
And you cannot go further
Than my sweet thoughts can go,
As they are with me always and
They are with you – and so
Even if I go to sleep,
Your picture's in my sight,
And it will wake my heart and to
My heart and eye's delight.

47

Betwixt mine eye and heart a league is took,
And each doth good turns now unto the other:
When that mine eye is famish'd for a look,
Or heart in love with sighs himself doth smother,
With my love's picture then my eye doth feast,
And to the painted banquet bids my heart;
Another time mine eye is my heart's guest,
And in his thoughts of love doth share a part:
So, either by thy picture or my love,
Thy self away, art present still with me;
For thou not farther than my thoughts canst move,
And I am still with them, and they with thee;
Or, if they sleep, thy picture in my sight
Awakes my heart, to heart's and eye's delight.

48

How carefully I did protect
These trivial things of mine,
Whenever I went travelling,
For I would thus confine
Each trifle under lock and key,
To make entirely sure,
That no false hand would steal my things
And mar my travel tour.
But you are worth much more, my love
Than all my petty things,
More valuable than lovely jewels,
Necklaces and rings,
Yet you – my consolation,
Cause me the utmost grief,
Because I worry you'll be prey
To every vulgar thief.
I haven't – cannot, lock you up
Within a heavy chest,
Except within the gentle realms
Of this my loving breast.
But you can go from there at will –
Leave me at any time –
And so I'm wont to fret I'll be
The victim of a crime,
That you'll be stolen from my breast,
For this I truly fear –
Even an honest man would steal
A prize that is so dear.

48

How careful was I when I took my way,
Each trifle under truest bars to thrust,
That to my use it might unused stay
From hands of falsehood, in sure wards of trust!
But thou, to whom my jewels trifles are,
Most worthy comfort, now my greatest grief,
Thou best of dearest, and mine only care,
Art left the prey of every vulgar thief.
Thee have I not lock'd up in any chest,
Save where thou art not, though I feel thou art,
Within the gentle closure of my breast,
From whence at pleasure thou mayst come and part;
And even thence thou wilt be stol'n I fear,
For truth proves thievish for a prize so dear.

49

In expectation of the time,
Should ever that time come,
When I will see you frown at me
With face severe and glum,
Which makes me ponder for a while,
As one who thus suspects,
Your love has run its course and now
You see all my defects.
When I anticipate the time
That you thus walk on by,
Just like a stranger passing,
And with a downcast eye,
With no sign of acknowledgement –
When your love's been converted
Into a settled gravity,
And our love's been perverted.
And in that future time I now
Accept what I am due,
For truthfully I don't deserve
To have the likes of you.
I offer up now no defence,
For it is surely so
That it's extremely reasonable
For you to lay me low.
To leave poor me – I understand,
It's common sense you see,
For it cannot be justified
That you're in love with me.

49

Against that time, if ever that time come,
When I shall see thee frown on my defects,
When as thy love hath cast his utmost sum,
Call'd to that audit by advis'd respects;
Against that time when thou shalt strangely pass,
And scarcely greet me with that sun, thine eye,
When love, converted from the thing it was,
Shall reasons find of settled gravity;
Against that time do I ensconce me here,
Within the knowledge of mine own desert,
And this my hand, against my self uprear,
To guard the lawful reasons on thy part:
    To leave poor me thou hast the strength of laws,
    Since why to love I can allege no cause.

50

How wearily I journey
Right from the very start,
I travel on with gloomy thoughts
And with a heavy heart.
And when I finally arrive
At my journey's end,
I know with time for rest and ease,
I'll think about my friend.
And I will be there so aware
And so devoid of smiles,
Because my friend is far away,
Across long, countless miles.
And the horse that bears me now
Seems tired by my woe,
He plods and bears the weight in me,
As if the wretch did know.
He seems to sense I'm leaving you
And so my special need,
Is not to travel quickly,
His rider loves not speed.
My bloody spur won't move him on
When thrust into his hide;
He only groans, which hurts me more
Than my spur hurts his side.
And that sad groan from my poor horse
Puts this thought in my mind;
All my grief lies onward,
My joy all lies behind.

50

How heavy do I journey on the way,
When what I seek, my weary travel's end,
Doth teach that ease and that repose to say,
'Thus far the miles are measured from thy friend!'
The beast that bears me, tired with my woe,
Plods dully on, to bear that weight in me,
As if by some instinct the wretch did know
His rider lov'd not speed, being made from thee:
The bloody spur cannot provoke him on,
That sometimes anger thrusts into his hide,
Which heavily he answers with a groan,
More sharp to me than spurring to his side;
For that same groan doth put this in my mind,
My grief lies onward, and my joy behind.

51

Thus does my love, make this excuse
For my poor horse's speed,
He plods along with head bowed down,
A dull but faithful steed.
And why should I make haste when it's
Not what I wish to do?
The only time to rush is when
I'm coming back to you.
So what excuse will my old horse
Make then? Well I don't know,
For however fast he runs
It still will seem too slow.
I'd spur him on, even if
He ran at fearsome pace,
And galloped like the very wind
As if in a great race.
And even if he flew as if
He had wings and the will
To overcome all obstacles,
I'd still think he stood still.
Therefore desire, formed from my love
For your most lovely face,
Will be just like a horse who's made
From fire and in a race.
But since when leaving you my horse
Went wilfully so slow,
On coming back, I'll run myself,
And give him leave to go.

51

Thus can my love excuse the slow offence
Of my dull bearer when from thee I speed:
From where thou art why should I haste me thence?
Till I return, of posting is no need.
O, what excuse will my poor beast then find,
When swift extremity can seem but slow?
Then should I spur, though mounted on the wind,
In winged speed no motion shall I know,
Then can no horse with my desire keep pace;
Therefore desire, of perfect'st love being made,
Shall neigh--no dull flesh--in his fiery race;
But love, for love, thus shall excuse my jade,--
'Since from thee going, he went wilful-slow,
Towards thee I'll run, and give him leave to go.'

52

I think I'm like a rich man
Who has a blessed key
To a treasure that's locked up
Which he then cannot see.
He doesn't wish to spoil the joy
Or dampen down his pleasure,
By gazing endlessly upon
All his lovely treasure.
It's like great feasts, if they were held
On every single day,
Why their familiarity
Would take the fun away.
That's why feast days are thinly spread
Across the whole, long year,
Like stones of worth in necklaces,
Placed apart – not near.
And time that keeps us separate
Is like my treasure chest,
Or wardrobe storing gorgeous robes –
For when displayed – I'm blest.
It makes the moment special
When they are all revealed,
A moment heightened by the fact
That they have been concealed.
And you are blessed with such a worth,
That those with you can see,
They're lucky – and those not with you
Hope that they soon will be.

52

So am I as the rich, whose blessed key,
Can bring him to his sweet up-locked treasure,
The which he will not every hour survey,
For blunting the fine point of seldom pleasure.
Therefore are feasts so solemn and so rare,
Since, seldom coming in that long year set,
Like stones of worth they thinly placed are,
Or captain jewels in the carcanet.
So is the time that keeps you as my chest,
Or as the wardrobe which the robe doth hide,
To make some special instant special-blest,
By new unfolding his imprison'd pride.
Blessed are you whose worthiness gives scope,
Being had, to triumph; being lacked, to hope.

53

What are your special assets
That you seem to accrue?
Those million strange shadows that
Make you uniquely you.
Most folk have but one image,
When all is said and done,
But though just one, you share a part
Of you – with everyone.
In trying to paint Adonis,
An artist would then do
An imitation that was poor –
Inferior to you.
And if he painted Helen,
Her beauty thus to seek,
He'd just end up in painting you
And dressed up as a Greek.
Give praise to spring and autumn,
And spring will only show,
A shadow of your beauty
That all have come to know.
And autumn never can compare
With all that you display,
It's never quite as wonderful
As you are every day.
In all that's beautiful in life,
You truly have a part,
And no-one can compare with you
And your dear, constant heart.

53

What is your substance, whereof are you made,
That millions of strange shadows on you tend?
Since every one, hath every one, one shade,
And you but one, can every shadow lend.
Describe Adonis, and the counterfeit
Is poorly imitated after you;
On Helen's cheek all art of beauty set,
And you in Grecian tires are painted new:
Speak of the spring, and foison of the year,
The one doth shadow of your beauty show,
The other as your bounty doth appear;
And you in every blessed shape we know.
In all external grace you have some part,
But you like none, none you, for constant heart.

54

How beautiful great beauty seems
When it's accompanied by,
The ornament of truthfulness –
It lights a dismal sky.
And roses too look wonderful
But weave a special spell,
For they're enhanced and greatly by
Their sweet and luscious smell.
And dog-roses, all growing wild,
As we pass on by,
Are just as colourful – and too,
Bring pleasure to the eye.
Like other roses they have thorns –
When summer comes along,
They spread their beauty all around
In colours soft and strong.
Their virtue's in their looks, but they're
An undervalued show,
For when they die they're just ignored
And no-one wants to know.
Sweet roses have a better fate,
Their beauty doesn't fade,
For when they die they live again,
For sweet perfumes are made.
And so with you, 'twill be the same,
Sweet and beauteous youth,
For when you fade away, my verse
Will then preserve your truth.

54

O, how much more doth beauty beauteous seem
By that sweet ornament which truth doth give.
The rose looks fair, but fairer we it deem
For that sweet odour, which doth in it live.
The canker blooms have full as deep a dye
As the perfumed tincture of the roses.
Hang on such thorns, and play as wantonly
When summer's breath their masked buds discloses:
But, for their virtue only is their show,
They live unwoo'd, and unrespected fade;
Die to themselves. Sweet roses do not so;
Of their sweet deaths, are sweetest odours made:
And so of you, beauteous and lovely youth,
When that shall vade, by verse distills your truth.

55

Not marble or gold monuments
Of princes – 'cross all time,
Will ever live for longer than
The power of my rhyme.
And you shall shine more brightly
Than stones – for they disperse –
For you will live forevermore,
Captured in this verse.
When wasteful war, great statues
Brings down and overturns,
When Mars, his sword clasped in his hand
Comes with the fire that burns,
When all of this shall come about,
The one thing we shall see
Is nothing will be then erased
Of your dear memory.
'Gainst death and stupid enmity,
You will still carry on,
You'll always be remembered,
A light will still be shone.
And praise will still be lavished,
As all will surely see,
Your worth will live within the eyes
Of all posterity.
So till the judgement's final doom,
When you yourself arise,
You'll live on in this verse and in
All sweet, young lover's eyes.

55

Not marble, nor the gilded monuments
Of princes, shall outlive this powerful rhyme;
But you shall shine more bright in these contents
Than unswept stone, besmear'd with sluttish time.
When wasteful war shall statues overturn,
And broils root out the work of masonry,
Nor Mars his sword, nor war's quick fire shall burn
The living record of your memory.
'Gainst death, and all-oblivious enmity
Shall you pace forth; your praise shall still find room
Even in the eyes of all posterity
That wear this world out to the ending doom.
So, till the judgment that yourself arise,
You live in this, and dwell in lovers' eyes.

56

Sweet love, sweet love, renew your strength,
Be just as strong as ever,
Don't let it e'er be said that lust
Is stronger – never, never.
For lustful appetite that's fed,
Today's put out of sight,
But tomorrow's back – and sharp –
And with its former might.
And so let love be just like this –
Although your hungry eyes
Are filled today and thus grow dull,
Tomorrow let love rise.
For it will be renewed again,
Love's spirit – do not kill,
Don't let perpetual dullness reign
Because you've had your fill.
Let the period of distance,
The separation be –
Like sandy shores that lie apart,
Divided by the sea.
And two young lovers daily come,
To see their love so true,
And they each feel they're doubly blessed
If their love comes in view.
Or else call this the winter time,
Which is both cold and raw,
Which makes us wish for summertime,
Then wish it three times more.

56

Sweet love, renew thy force; be it not said
Thy edge should blunter be than appetite,
Which but to-day by feeding is allay'd,
To-morrow sharpened in his former might:
So, love, be thou, although to-day thou fill
Thy hungry eyes, even till they wink with fullness,
To-morrow see again, and do not kill
The spirit of love, with a perpetual dullness.
Let this sad interim like the ocean be
Which parts the shore, where two contracted new
Come daily to the banks, that when they see
Return of love, more blest may be the view;
Or call it winter, which being full of care,
Makes summer's welcome, thrice more wished, more rare.

57

Because I am your slave, I ask
Whatever should I do?
Just wait around for hours and hours
Until time's right for you.
I have no precious time to spend
And nothing I desire,
No services to do until
There's something you require.
Nor dare I thus berate the world,
While I, my sovereign, view
The time just slowly ticking by
And watch the clock for you.
Nor should I think and bitterly
At how your absence grates,
Even though your sad farewell
Is what your servant hates.
Nor dare I question you, and with
My silly, jealous thought,
'What do you do?' – then like a slave
I stay and think of nought,
Except of course, how happy
You make those lucky few,
With whom you spend the passing hours,
Who know just what you do.
Such a fool is faithful love,
That what e'er your will,
Though you do anything you like,
He still thinks you no ill.

57

Being your slave what should I do but tend,
Upon the hours, and times of your desire?
I have no precious time at all to spend;
Nor services to do, till you require.
Nor dare I chide the world-without-end hour,
Whilst I, my sovereign, watch the clock for you,
Nor think the bitterness of absence sour,
When you have bid your servant once adieu;
Nor dare I question with my jealous thought
Where you may be, or your affairs suppose,
But, like a sad slave, stay and think of nought
Save, where you are, how happy you make those.
So true a fool is love, that in your will,
Though you do anything, he thinks no ill.

58

That god that made me be your slave,
Let him not let me be
Demanding thus, because I think
You should spend time with me.
Or think that you should give account
Of how you pass the hours,
I must recall, I am your slave
And you hold all the powers.
I am your vassal, it is true –
Whatever may befall,
I must remember that I am
Here at your beck and call.
So let me suffer patiently,
Till your longed for return,
As you fulfil your every wish –
My company you spurn.
I'll suffer all and quietly,
Without accusing you,
Of causing me an injury
In all you choose to do.
Go where you will, it is your right,
Do what you will with time,
And you can grant a pardon to
Yourself for any crime.
For it's my role to wait around
Till you've consumed your fill,
And not to blame you for your acts,
Be they for good or ill.

58

That god forbid, that made me first your slave,
I should in thought control your times of pleasure,
Or at your hand the account of hours to crave,
Being your vassal, bound to stay your leisure!
O, let me suffer, being at your beck,
The imprison'd absence of your liberty;
And patience, tame to sufferance, bide each check,
Without accusing you of injury.
Be where you list, your charter is so strong
That you yourself may privilege your time
To what you will; to you it doth belong
Yourself to pardon of self-doing crime.
I am to wait, though waiting so be hell,
Not blame your pleasure be it ill or well.

59

If there is nothing new, but just
What has been here before,
And if we see as in the past
What all those others saw,
How can we urge our brains to write
Some words that are brand new?
We're likely copying a thought
That others copied too.
After painful labour then
An imitation's born,
And this was also taken from
Another – old and worn.
I wish I could go back in time,
Five hundred years – and look,
To see your image written in
Some ancient, antique book.
And then I'd see what that old world
Had at that time to say,
About your lovely shape and form,
And then I'd see the way
They wrote – on those long, far off days,
And what would be their claim,
Did they write better – worse than us?
Or did they write the same.
I'm sure that writers with great wit,
Who wrote in former days,
Have given to those worse than you
The same admiring praise.

59

If there be nothing new, but that which is
Hath been before, how are our brains beguil'd,
Which labouring for invention bear amiss
The second burthen of a former child!
O, that record could with a backward look,
Even of five hundred courses of the sun,
Show me your image in some antique book,
Since mind at first in character was done!
That I might see what the old world could say
To this composed wonder of your frame;
Whether we are mended, or wh'er better they,
Or whether revolution be the same.
O, sure I am the wits of former days,
To subjects worse have given admiring praise.

60

As breaking waves move on towards
The lovely pebbled shore,
So do our minutes hasten to
When we will be no more.
Each moment changes places with
The one before to spend
The time in moving onwards –
Towards that certain end.
And each thing born within this world –
Although once found to be
In that pure light before its birth –
Crawls to maturity.
And there it finds as it moves on,
In its own life story,
Such merciless, harsh obstacles,
That fight against its glory.
And Time that lavishes great gifts,
Those gifts, now disavows,
It takes the beauty set on youth,
Puts wrinkles on their brows.
It takes the best of nature's best,
It lays all down so low,
There's nothing in the whole, wide world
That its sharp scythe won't mow.
And yet my verse will persevere,
And will forever stand,
To praise your worth and excellence
Despite Time's cruel, hard hand.

60

Like as the waves make towards the pebbled shore,
So do our minutes hasten to their end;
Each changing place with that which goes before,
In sequent toil all forwards do contend.
Nativity, once in the main of light,
Crawls to maturity, wherewith being crown'd,
Crooked eclipses 'gainst his glory fight,
And Time that gave doth now his gift confound.
Time doth transfix the flourish set on youth
And delves the parallels in beauty's brow,
Feeds on the rarities of nature's truth,
And nothing stands but for his scythe to mow:
And yet to times in hope, my verse shall stand.
Praising thy worth, despite his cruel hand.

61

So what is your objective?
That I spend every night
Taunted by your image as
It flits across my sight.
Is it that you just wish that I
Lie with eyes wide open,
Thinking of you endlessly,
And with my slumber broken.
Do you thus send your spirit
To pry and spy to see
What shameful deeds, in idle hours
Have captivated me?
Does this mean you are jealous? No.
For though you love me much,
Your love is not so great that you
Do hunger for my touch.
It's my great love for you that keeps
Me in my bed awake,
I play the watchman, worrying,
And always for your sake.
And so I keep a watch because
I do so deeply care,
And while I do, it's my belief,
That you're awake elsewhere.
Far from me, a long way off,
But I have cause to fear
That you're with other people who
Are really all too near.

61

Is it thy will, thy image should keep open
My heavy eyelids to the weary night?
Dost thou desire my slumbers should be broken,
While shadows like to thee do mock my sight?
Is it thy spirit that thou send'st from thee
So far from home into my deeds to pry,
To find out shames and idle hours in me,
The scope and tenure of thy jealousy?
O, no! thy love, though much, is not so great:
It is my love that keeps mine eye awake:
Mine own true love that doth my rest defeat,
To play the watchman ever for thy sake:
For thee watch I, whilst thou dost wake elsewhere,
From me far off, with others all too near.

62

I am possessed by a great sin,
Which I think is above
All other sins, for I'm possessed
With that gross sin – self love.
It dominates my very soul
And every part of me,
And there's no way to cure myself,
For there's no remedy.
It's embedded in my heart –
For there's no face like mine,
My body is a perfect shape,
Upright, strong and fine.
My character is of such worth,
That when it's all unfurled,
I do believe it's finer than
All others in this world.
And so in short I am convinced
That I stand very tall,
And I eclipse all others so
I'm better than them all.
But when into the mirror
I look – it's then I see,
A beaten, old and battered face,
Worn out and elderly.
Self love's a sin – it's really you,
I praise when I self praise,
I decorate my age and with
The beauty of your days.

62

Sin of self-love possesseth all mine eye
And all my soul, and all my every part;
And for this sin there is no remedy,
It is so grounded inward in my heart.
Methinks no face so gracious is as mine,
No shape so true, no truth of such account;
And for myself mine own worth do define,
As I all other in all worths surmount.
But when my glass shows me myself indeed
Beated and chopp'd with tanned antiquity,
Mine own self-love quite contrary I read;
Self so self-loving were iniquity.
'Tis thee,--myself,--that for myself I praise,
Painting my age with beauty of thy days.

63

In expectation of the time,
Of when my love shall bow
To Time's pernicious, crushing hand,
And be as I am now;
When hours and years have drained his blood,
His body's tired and worn,
When lines and wrinkles etch his face –
And his bright, youthful morn
Has travelled on remorselessly,
To age's cold, dark night,
And all those beauties he now has
Have disappeared from sight.
When in that time when he will lose
His looks and everything,
And nature steals his youthful days –
The treasure of his spring,
Against the future time to be,
That comes to every life,
I now defend myself against
Age's cruel, sharp knife.
For Time shall never take from me
The memory, so true
Of my love's beauty, though Time takes
His life and all he knew.
And so his beauty, in these lines
Will be forever sung,
And these my lines, they will live on
And keep him ever young.

63

Against my love shall be as I am now,
With Time's injurious hand crush'd and o'erworn;
When hours have drain'd his blood and fill'd his brow
With lines and wrinkles; when his youthful morn
Hath travell'd on to age's steepy night;
And all those beauties whereof now he's king
Are vanishing, or vanished out of sight,
Stealing away the treasure of his spring;
For such a time do I now fortify
Against confounding age's cruel knife,
That he shall never cut from memory
My sweet love's beauty, though my lover's life:
His beauty shall in these black lines be seen,
And they shall live, and he in them still green.

64

When I have seen Time's awful hand
Deface great buildings – when,
I've seen destroyed, the monuments
To ancient, buried men.
When I've seen lofty towers fall down,
And seen mere mortals rage,
And then eradicate hard brass
That has been there an age.
When I've seen the hungry ocean,
Engulf and take the shore,
So that a part of the lush land
Is gone forevermore.
Or when the firm soil of the coast
Eats up the watery main,
So that the loss of one of them
Is then the others gain.
When I have seen the interchange
With one state borne away,
Converted to another, or
To rot and then decay.
Why all this ruin that's around
Has made me ruminate,
And think that Time will take my love,
And leave me in a state.
This thought is like a death to me,
A thing I cannot choose,
But it just makes me weep to think
Of what I fear to lose.

64

When I have seen by Time's fell hand defac'd
The rich-proud cost of outworn buried age;
When sometime lofty towers I see down-raz'd,
And brass eternal slave to mortal rage;
When I have seen the hungry ocean gain
Advantage on the kingdom of the shore,
And the firm soil win of the watery main,
Increasing store with loss, and loss with store;
When I have seen such interchange of state,
Or state itself confounded, to decay;
Ruin hath taught me thus to ruminate--
That Time will come and take my love away.
This thought is as a death which cannot choose
But weep to have, that which it fears to lose.

65

Since burnished brass, nor stone, nor earth,
Nor the boundless sea,
Has the power to fight against
Sad mortality,
Then how can beauty fight against,
Or ever have the powers,
To hold off death, when all its strength
Is no more than a flower's?
However could your beauty,
Which is like summer's breath,
Hold out against the siege of time
That brings with it cold death.
For solid granite rock and too
Massive gates of steel,
Are not themselves so strong that they
Don't come in time to feel,
The great decaying power of time:
Oh fear. Alack. Alack.
Where can I hide your beauty,
To hold Time's swift foot back?
Who has a hand that's strong enough?
Or when their will's uncoiled,
Has the ability to see
Your beauty's never spoiled.
Well no-one – but a miracle
Somehow then just might,
For through the black ink of my verse
My love may still shine bright.

65

Since brass, nor stone, nor earth, nor boundless sea,
But sad mortality o'ersways their power,
How with this rage shall beauty hold a plea,
Whose action is no stronger than a flower?
O, how shall summer's honey breath hold out,
Against the wrackful siege of battering days,
When rocks impregnable are not so stout,
Nor gates of steel so strong but Time decays?
O fearful meditation! where, alack,
Shall Time's best jewel from Time's chest lie hid?
Or what strong hand can hold his swift foot back?
Or who his spoil of beauty can forbid?
O, none, unless this miracle have might,
That in black ink my love may still shine bright.

66

Because I'm tired of many things
That cause me thus to sigh,
It must be said and honestly,
For restful death I cry.
I've had enough of just too much –
Like decent people born
To be poor beggars in the street –
To folk that we should scorn,
Who're dressed up in frivolity –
To promises not kept –
And honour shamefully bestowed
On people who're inept.
And maidens rudely turned to whores,
And people in the right,
Wrongfully disgraced and viewed
Badly in men's sight.
And the strong, disabled thus
By those in power who're weak,
And art made tongue-tied by these powers,
They miss what artists seek.
And fools in charge of wise men,
And simple truths denied,
And evil overtaking good,
Around us far and wide.
I'm tired with all these rotten things,
And I must up and own,
I'd like to die, save for the fact,
I'd leave my love alone.

66

Tired with all these, for restful death I cry,
As to behold desert a beggar born,
And needy nothing trimm'd in jollity,
And purest faith unhappily forsworn,
And gilded honour shamefully misplac'd,
And maiden virtue rudely strumpeted,
And right perfection wrongfully disgrac'd,
And strength by limping sway disabled
And art made tongue-tied by authority,
And folly--doctor-like--controlling skill,
And simple truth miscall'd simplicity,
And captive good attending captain ill:
Tir'd with all these, from these would I be gone,
Save that, to die, I leave my love alone.

67

Why should the man I love be thus
Infected – I do pray –
By sinners who corrupt the world,
Why should he live this way?
And from his presence they obtain
Advantage – for we see
They gain a lift by knowing him –
From his society.
And why should painters imitate
His lovely features – when
They cannot catch the beauty of
This handsomest of men?
And why should those less beautiful
Do all thus to pursue
To be a rose – when only he
Can be a rose that's true?
And why should he now live at all
When Nature is so fazed,
She can't put blood through lively veins,
Her vigour is erased?
She has no fund of beauty now
Except what lives in him,
And so to borrow from his store
Becomes fair Natures whim.
But let her keep him thus alive
To show what wealth she had,
In days gone by, so long ago,
Before the days went bad.

67

Ah! wherefore with infection should he live,
And with his presence grace impiety,
That sin by him advantage should achieve,
And lace itself with his society?
Why should false painting imitate his cheek,
And steel dead seeming of his living hue?
Why should poor beauty indirectly seek
Roses of shadow, since his rose is true?
Why should he live, now Nature bankrupt is,
Beggar'd of blood to blush through lively veins?
For she hath no exchequer now but his,
And proud of many, lives upon his gains.
O, him she stores, to show what wealth she had
In days long since, before these last so bad.

68

Thus is his face the map of days,
Long worn and now gone by,
When lovely people lived their lives
And would as surely die.
They lived and died as flowers do now,
And this was all before
False signs of beauty were thus born,
And long before we saw
Them placed on people's brows – before
Gold tresses of the dead
Were shorn from corpses – made to live
Upon a second head.
This was before those lovely locks,
That in a grave should be,
Were used to give another joy
By wearing merrily.
In him a natural beauty
Can readily be seen,
Without false ornament and thus
Honest and serene.
No stealing someone else's youth,
He has a look that's true,
No robbing from the old to then
Dress his looks anew.
And Nature keeps him as a map,
Within her treasured store,
To show the art of making up
What beauty was before.

68

Thus is his cheek the map of days outworn,
When beauty lived and died as flowers do now,
Before these bastard signs of fair were born,
Or durst inhabit on a living brow;
Before the golden tresses of the dead,
The right of sepulchres, were shorn away,
To live a second life on second head;
Ere beauty's dead fleece made another gay:
In him those holy antique hours are seen,
Without all ornament, itself and true,
Making no summer of another's green,
Robbing no old to dress his beauty new;
And him as for a map doth Nature store,
To show false Art what beauty was of yore.

69

Those parts of you that can be viewed
By the world's keen eye,
Could never be made better
However hard folk try.
Your beauty could not be improved,
You lack for nothing – so
It's something that the world admits,
It's what they've come to know.
It is the stark and honest truth,
Even foes praise you,
They only utter words that are
Completely fair and true.
The outward you receives much praise,
But looking in your mind,
Some people take a different view,
For in your mind they find,
A different you – they judge you then
By actions that you do,
And through these deeds they come to see
Quite another you.
Though outside you look beautiful,
The measure of your deeds
Shows though you smell like flowers outside,
Inside you smell like weeds.
The reason that your inside smells,
And doesn't match your show,
Is because you're spending time
With folk not good to know.

69

Those parts of thee that the world's eye doth view
Want nothing that the thought of hearts can mend;
All tongues--the voice of souls--give thee that due,
Uttering bare truth, even so as foes commend.
Thy outward thus with outward praise is crown'd;
But those same tongues, that give thee so thine own,
In other accents do this praise confound
By seeing farther than the eye hath shown.
They look into the beauty of thy mind,
And that in guess they measure by thy deeds;
Then--churls--their thoughts, although their eyes were kind,
To thy fair flower add the rank smell of weeds:
But why thy odour matcheth not thy show,
The soil is this, that thou dost common grow.

70

That you are slandered, often blamed,
And bad things said of you,
Will not be held against you for
It's just what people do.
For people who are beautiful
Draw treatment that's unfair,
Suspected like a large, black crow
In heaven's sweetest air.
For when you're acting well you'll be
Targeted and more,
When in your prime, pure and unstained,
You'll be ambushed for sure.
Just like a canker does devour
The sweetest buds of all,
So it is, that critics thus
With zeal, upon you fall.
You've avoided many pitfalls
That young men often find,
Because nobody tempted you
Or through your strength of mind.
And even though I praise you much,
It won't stop talk that's ill,
For people will show envy
And sadly always will.
If some suspicion of your good
Had not been thus unfurled,
You'd be the most loved person
Within the whole wide world.

70

That thou art blam'd shall not be thy defect,
For slander's mark was ever yet the fair;
The ornament of beauty is suspect,
A crow that flies in heaven's sweetest air.
So thou be good, slander doth but approve
Thy worth the greater being woo'd of time;
For canker vice the sweetest buds doth love,
And thou present'st a pure unstained prime.
Thou hast passed by the ambush of young days
Either not assail'd, or victor being charg'd;
Yet this thy praise cannot be so thy praise,
To tie up envy, evermore enlarg'd,
If some suspect of ill mask'd not thy show,
Then thou alone kingdoms of hearts shouldst owe.

71

When you hear the certain news
That I am truly dead,
Have left forever this sad world
And that my soul has fled.
Well mourn me then, for just as long
As the funeral bell
Rings out to give a warning that
Now with vile worms I dwell.
And if you read these words, forget
The hand that wrote this line,
For I love you so very much,
And though you were once mine,
There is one thing I wouldn't wish –
I would not want to know,
That when I died you then were filled
With sadness and with woe.
I say that if you read my verse
When I'm wrapped up in clay,
Do not so much as say my name,
Let love, like life, decay.
For if you do remember me,
The world will ask you why
You are so sad and sorrowful,
Why do you sigh and cry?
And when they find the reason,
They'll use my memory
To mock you and make fun of you –
And this should never be.

71

No longer mourn for me when I am dead
Than you shall hear the surly sullen bell
Give warning to the world that I am fled
From this vile world with vilest worms to dwell:
Nay, if you read this line, remember not
The hand that writ it, for I love you so,
That I in your sweet thoughts would be forgot,
If thinking on me then should make you woe.
O, if,--I say you look upon this verse,
When I perhaps compounded am with clay,
Do not so much as my poor name rehearse;
But let your love even with my life decay;
Lest the wise world should look into your moan,
And mock you with me after I am gone.

72

And if the world should then desire,
That you, dear love, recite
The merit I possessed, why don't,
For it would not be right.
Once I'm dead, forget me for
There's nothing good to say
About my life and who I was,
So let it rest I pray.
There's nothing worthy can be said,
Unless you lie and then,
Make it sound as if I was
One of those better men,
And hang more praise on my dead self
Than truly I deserve,
In an attempt, because of love
A good name to preserve.
So when my body's buried,
Let also be my name,
So that it can no longer bring
To you or me great shame.
For I'm ashamed of what I bring,
What out of me does come,
And you should also feel the same,
Make sure you don't succumb
To saying words that are untrue,
Just out of love and so,
When I'm gone it's best that you
Forget – just let me go.

72

O, lest the world should task you to recite
What merit lived in me, that you should love
After my death,--dear love, forget me quite,
For you in me can nothing worthy prove;
Unless you would devise some virtuous lie,
To do more for me than mine own desert,
And hang more praise upon deceased I
Than niggard truth would willingly impart:
O, lest your true love may seem false in this
That you for love speak well of me untrue,
My name be buried where my body is,
And live no more to shame nor me nor you.
For I am shamed by that which I bring forth,
And so should you, to love things nothing worth.

73

When you see me, you can behold
That dismal time of year,
When yellow leaves have fallen and
There is but little cheer.
Or when trees are completely bare –
Where sweet birds sang before,
We now can see those selfsame birds
Shivering to the core.
In me you see the twilight
Of a dying day
Which after sunset, the black night
Does quickly take away.
And this black night that takes the day's
Last and final breath,
Is like death's twin that seals up all
Within eternal death.
In me you see the glowing fire
That on its ashes lie,
Consuming there the very thing
That it was nourished by.
It seems as if it lies atop
Its very own death bed,
And so it makes you realise
One day you will be dead.
You see all this and it does make
Your love appear more strong,
For you love most when you know well,
You'll leave before too long.

73

That time of year thou mayst in me behold
When yellow leaves, or none, or few, do hang
Upon those boughs which shake against the cold,
Bare ruin'd choirs, where late the sweet birds sang.
In me thou see'st the twilight of such day
As after sunset fadeth in the west;
Which by and by black night doth take away,
Death's second self, that seals up all in rest.
In me thou see'st the glowing of such fire,
That on the ashes of his youth doth lie,
As the death-bed, whereon it must expire,
Consum'd with that which it was nourish'd by.
This thou perceiv'st, which makes thy love more strong,
To love that well, which thou must leave ere long.

74

Be not unhappy when I die,
When I thus go away,
It's like arrest but with no bail
Allowed on any day.
For no-one is released from death,
But in a way I'll be
Still with you through my humble lines,
So you'll remember me.
And when you read these words of mine,
And once again review
The very part of me that was
Committed just to you,
You'll see again how much I loved,
And how the common earth
Can only have my earthly part
For you keep my true worth.
And so you own my better part,
My spirit is all yours;
The earth still has my body which
Succumbed to death's grim jaws.
It is now the prey of worms,
The part that death could kill,
The part not worth remembering – yet
My spirit's with you still.
For it lives on within my verse
And all that it contains,
And so through this I'll be with you –
The real me still remains.

74

But be contented: when that fell arrest
Without all bail shall carry me away,
My life hath in this line some interest,
Which for memorial still with thee shall stay.
When thou reviewest this, thou dost review
The very part was consecrate to thee:
The earth can have but earth, which is his due;
My spirit is thine, the better part of me:
So then thou hast but lost the dregs of life,
The prey of worms, my body being dead;
The coward conquest of a wretch's knife,
Too base of thee to be remembered.
The worth of that is that which it contains,
And that is this, and this with thee remains.

75

You are to me, as food to life,
My world needs you around,
To me you're like soft showers to
The flowers in the ground.
And only you can give me peace
And keep me in good health.
I struggle like a miser fights
'Twixt himself and wealth.
Sometimes his fortune he enjoys,
It brings him boundless pleasure,
And then he worries that a thief
Will make off with his treasure.
Sometimes I think that I prefer
To be alone with you,
And then I think the world should see
My joy in all we do.
Sometimes I feel I've overfed –
Feasting on your sight,
And other times I'm starving for
One look for my delight.
And I can have no joy in life
Except that which you give,
Or that which I thus take from you –
They both help me to live.
And so I yearn for you some days –
Then overdo your touch,
I either don't see you enough
Or else see you too much.

75

So are you to my thoughts as food to life,
Or as sweet-season'd showers are to the ground;
And for the peace of you I hold such strife
As 'twixt a miser and his wealth is found.
Now proud as an enjoyer, and anon
Doubting the filching age will steal his treasure;
Now counting best to be with you alone,
Then better'd that the world may see my pleasure:
Sometime all full with feasting on your sight,
And by and by clean starved for a look;
Possessing or pursuing no delight,
Save what is had, or must from you be took.
Thus do I pine and surfeit day by day,
Or gluttoning on all, or all away.

76

Why is my verse so commonplace?
It's barren of fresh style,
It lacks a great variety,
It's dull – and by a mile.
Why don't I take the time to look
At what those others do?
Those writers who attempt to write
With a style that's new.
Why do I seem to write such things
That always are the same?
The words are so predictable,
They almost tell my name.
The words show every reader
Just who gave them birth,
Exactly where they came from so
They can thus judge my worth.
You should know, sweet love of mine,
I always write of you,
So all I do is take old words
And dress them up as new.
I spend those words again although
They are already spent,
And it is like the warming sun
Which is daily sent.
For as the sun is every day
New and then it's old,
So my love simply makes me tell
What I've already told.

76

Why is my verse so barren of new pride,
So far from variation or quick change?
Why with the time do I not glance aside
To new-found methods, and to compounds strange?
Why write I still all one, ever the same,
And keep invention in a noted weed,
That every word doth almost tell my name,
Showing their birth, and where they did proceed?
O, know sweet love I always write of you,
And you and love are still my argument;
So all my best is dressing old words new,
Spending again what is already spent:
For as the sun is daily new and old,
So is my love still telling what is told.

77

If you look in the mirror
You'll see how you are faring;
The glass will show you clearly
That your beauty's wearing.
Your clock will show time's moving on,
Each day it wastes away,
But in this book, you can then write
Your thoughts on every day.
And from these thoughts you'll surely learn –
Such things you'll come to know,
For when into your glass you look,
And that true glass does show
Your wrinkled face there looking back –
Then from your memory
You'll think of open mouthed, dark graves,
And then eternity.
For your clock's dial, with shady stealth,
Moves on and steals your prime,
So to preserve it, write your thoughts,
To have them for all time.
And when you read in future years
These children of your brain,
They will have grown, you'll treasure all
That they then contain.
These actions done and frequently –
If often you will look –
Will be a benefit to you
And much enrich your book.

77

Thy glass will show thee how thy beauties wear,
Thy dial how thy precious minutes waste;
These vacant leaves thy mind's imprint will bear,
And of this book, this learning mayst thou taste.
The wrinkles which thy glass will truly show
Of mouthed graves will give thee memory;
Thou by thy dial's shady stealth mayst know
Time's thievish progress to eternity.
Look! what thy memory cannot contain,
Commit to these waste blanks, and thou shalt find
Those children nursed, deliver'd from thy brain,
To take a new acquaintance of thy mind.
These offices, so oft as thou wilt look,
Shall profit thee and much enrich thy book.

78

Now that I have so often
Invoked you as my Muse,
It has encouraged others
To do the same and choose
To write their verse about you;
They all do as I do,
They use their alien pens to write
Their poems just to you.
Your eyes have taught the dumb to sing,
Caused ignorance to fly,
And taught the clever folk to soar
Much higher in the sky.
You've given graceful people
A double dose of grace,
And yet your greatest pride should be,
And really is the case,
That you have caused me thus to write –
And everything I do
Is influenced by your sweet self,
And inspired by you.
In other writers work you just
Improve their given style,
And add a certain extra touch
That truly does beguile.
But with me – you're all my art
And art in me instil,
Without you I am ignorant
And lacking in all skill.

78

So oft have I invoked thee for my Muse,
And found such fair assistance in my verse
As every alien pen hath got my use
And under thee their poesy disperse.
Thine eyes, that taught the dumb on high to sing
And heavy ignorance aloft to fly,
Have added feathers to the learned's wing
And given grace a double majesty.
Yet be most proud of that which I compile,
Whose influence is thine, and born of thee:
In others' works thou dost but mend the style,
And arts with thy sweet graces graced be;
But thou art all my art, and dost advance
As high as learning, my rude ignorance.

79

When I alone wrote of you,
When it was only me
That wrote about your gentle grace
For other folk to see,
Why then I had the benefit
Of writing on my own,
But now my poems aren't so good
And I don't work alone.
And I accept that you deserve
A writer who can then,
Describe your beauty properly
And wield a worthier pen.
Yet while another poet
Writes of you – it's plain,
He only robs from you and then
He gives it back again.
He says that you are virtuous
But really stole that word
From watching how you act and all
That with you has occurred.
He states that you are beautiful,
But it is just the case,
He only saw your beauty
By looking at your face.
So don't thank him for his comments
And all he has to say,
For everything he gives to you –
He makes quite sure you pay.

79

Whilst I alone did call upon thy aid,
My verse alone had all thy gentle grace;
But now my gracious numbers are decay'd,
And my sick Muse doth give an other place.
I grant, sweet love, thy lovely argument
Deserves the travail of a worthier pen;
Yet what of thee thy poet doth invent
He robs thee of, and pays it thee again.
He lends thee virtue, and he stole that word
From thy behaviour; beauty doth he give,
And found it in thy cheek: he can afford
No praise to thee, but what in thee doth live.
Then thank him not for that which he doth say,
Since what he owes thee, thou thyself dost pay.

80

I get really quite upset
And feel it isn't right,
When I pick up my pen these days
About you thus to write –
To know a better writer
Does everything I do,
But makes a far superior job
When he's describing you.
He uses all his expertise
When praising your sweet name,
Which makes me feel quite tongue-tied
When writing of your fame.
And though upon the ocean
His proud, tall ship is borne
Along with my unworthy craft,
So small and so forlorn,
Yet still my boat sails wilfully
And keeps me then afloat,
While he rides out across the depths,
I'm in my little boat.
And if I'm wrecked, well so be it,
For it should be avowed,
Mine is but a worthless boat
Whilst his is tall and proud.
And if he thrives and for my sins
I am cast away –
I perished for my love is then
The worst thing you can say.

80

O, how I faint when I of you do write,
Knowing a better spirit doth use your name,
And in the praise thereof spends all his might,
To make me tongue-tied speaking of your fame!
But since your worth--wide as the ocean is,--
The humble as the proudest sail doth bear,
My saucy bark, inferior far to his,
On your broad main doth wilfully appear.
Your shallowest help will hold me up afloat,
Whilst he upon your soundless deep doth ride;
Or, being wrack'd, I am a worthless boat,
He of tall building, and of goodly pride:
Then if he thrive and I be cast away,
The worst was this,--my love was my decay.

81

Either I shall live to write
Your epitaph – or you
Will survive – when in the earth
I'm rotting through and through.
Death can never take away
Your sweet memory,
Though when I die, death will then take
Every part of me.
Your name will live for evermore,
But to the world I'll die,
When I am planted in the earth,
And in my coffin lie.
I'll be given just a grave
That's common – maybe worse,
But you'll receive a monument,
For it will be my verse.
And eyes not yet created
Will read – both old and young,
And people in the future time
Will speak with eager tongue.
And so this, my loving verse
Will with esteem be read,
When all the current breathers
In the world are dead.
For you shall live forever through
The virtue of my pen,
In the breath and from the mouths
Of the future's men.

81

Or I shall live your epitaph to make,
Or you survive when I in earth am rotten;
From hence your memory death cannot take,
Although in me each part will be forgotten.
Your name from hence immortal life shall have,
Though I, once gone, to all the world must die:
The earth can yield me but a common grave,
When you entombed in men's eyes shall lie.
Your monument shall be my gentle verse,
Which eyes not yet created shall o'er-read;
And tongues to be, your being shall rehearse,
When all the breathers of this world are dead;
You still shall live,--such virtue hath my pen,--
Where breath most breathes, even in the mouths of men.

82

I freely grant, that you were not
Married to my Muse.
You sometimes didn't really like
The words I chose to use.
And so it's fair to overlook
The fact you sometimes read
The poems that some others write,
For this I will concede,
That as you're very beautiful,
And this you surely know,
It's only fair they write of you,
That they should have their go.
For you know I am limited
In all that I can do,
I cannot write the poetry
Of writers who are new.
Yet though these modern writers have
Devised a lovely style,
And write such fancy rhetoric
That entertains a while,
You would be better served indeed
If your beauty were thus penned,
In plain and sympathetic words
By your truth-telling friend.
And their gross words would surely be
Much better implemented,
If they were used for those in need
To be thus complimented.

82

I grant thou wert not married to my Muse,
And therefore mayst without attaint o'erlook
The dedicated words which writers use
Of their fair subject, blessing every book.
Thou art as fair in knowledge as in hue,
Finding thy worth a limit past my praise;
And therefore art enforced to seek anew
Some fresher stamp of the time-bettering days.
And do so, love; yet when they have devis'd,
What strained touches rhetoric can lend,
Thou truly fair, wert truly sympathis'd
In true plain words, by thy true-telling friend;
And their gross painting might be better us'd
Where cheeks need blood; in thee it is abus'd.

83

I never thought you needed
To be praised – and thus,
I never quite went overboard,
I never made a fuss.
I never thought a poet
Could give you your true due,
That he could ever capture
The real and lovely you.
And therefore I've been tardy
And haven't tried to strive,
To catch your beauty in my verse
While you are still alive.
For all can see by looking
And come to surely know,
How much lovelier you are
Than my poor pen could show.
You thought my silence was a sin,
But I thought it my duty,
For by this act I in no way
Did impair your beauty.
But other writers praise you,
They try to bring you life,
But all they do is paint a tomb
That just brings on great strife.
For you possess more life within
One of your fair eyes,
Than all the poets in the world
Could in their praise devise.

83

I never saw that you did painting need,
And therefore to your fair no painting set;
I found, or thought I found, you did exceed
That barren tender of a poet's debt:
And therefore have I slept in your report,
That you yourself, being extant, well might show
How far a modern quill doth come too short,
Speaking of worth, what worth in you doth grow.
This silence for my sin you did impute,
Which shall be most my glory being dumb;
For I impair not beauty being mute,
When others would give life, and bring a tomb.
There lives more life in one of your fair eyes
Than both your poets can in praise devise.

84

Who is it writes about you most?
Which writer could say more?
For you alone are you and keep
Such beauty in your store.
Nobody can compare – and with
The beauty that you own,
Only you can be compared
With you – and you alone.
Even an unworthy pen
Can tell a little story,
And lend his subject something good
To improve their glory.
But he that writes of you will then
Only have to tell
Of the beauty you possess,
That in your face does dwell.
If he describes you as you are,
What nature made so fine,
His writing skill will be admired
And praised for every line.
But you bring down such curses
Upon yourself and for
The joy you have in hearing praise,
For writers then write more.
And then they try to flatter you,
And thus they write such verse,
That overdoes their praise for you
And so write verse that's worse.

84

Who is it that says most, which can say more,
Than this rich praise,--that you alone, are you?
In whose confine immured is the store
Which should example where your equal grew.
Lean penury within that pen doth dwell
That to his subject lends not some small glory;
But he that writes of you, if he can tell
That you are you, so dignifies his story,
Let him but copy what in you is writ,
Not making worse what nature made so clear,
And such a counterpart shall fame his wit,
Making his style admired every where.
You to your beauteous blessings add a curse,
Being fond on praise, which makes your praises worse.

85

My tongue-tied verse stays silent
While praise of you runs rife,
Capturing your character
And praising your blessed life.
Those others write with golden pens,
And muses are compiled,
And precious phrases written down
Are by these poets filed.
I think good thoughts about you whilst
Some write good words – and then,
Like an untutored clerk I cry
A fulsome, loud 'Amen',
To every verse that does come forth,
That offers praise to you,
I cry on hearing of your praise,
'It's so, it's really true.'
I marvel at the polished pens
And all their skilful ways,
And add a little of my own
To their deserving praise.
But what I add is something more,
For in my heart I know,
That though I speak much less than them,
I truly love you so.
And though I love you more, you should
Respect those others too
For their words – but judge me by
My thoughts and what I do.

85

My tongue-tied Muse in manners holds her still,
While comments of your praise richly compil'd,
Reserve their character with golden quill,
And precious phrase by all the Muses fil'd.
I think good thoughts, whilst others write good words,
And like unlettered clerk still cry 'Amen'
To every hymn that able spirit affords,
In polish'd form of well-refined pen.
Hearing you praised, I say "tis so, 'tis true,'
And to the most of praise add something more;
But that is in my thought, whose love to you,
Though words come hindmost, holds his rank before.
Then others, for the breath of words respect,
Me for my dumb thoughts, speaking in effect.

86

Was it that other poet's verse,
Written with such verve,
That caused me not to write my own,
And took away my nerve?
For as my thoughts did ripen in
Imagination's womb,
They quickly were destroyed by him,
Consigned thus to a tomb.
Now is his talent aided by
Past writers that he's read
That make him write so very well
And strikes this poet dead.
Why have I been thus silenced,
Have spirits come to him
And helped him with his writing? No.
This is an idle whim.
Neither he nor night time spirits
Or friendly little ghost,
Can say they silenced me – or thus
In any form then boast,
That they have caused my silence
Whenever they are near,
That I can't write a single word
Because I'm sick with fear.
What silenced me – was your delight
In my rival's every line;
It helped him write much better verse,
Whilst it enfeebled mine.

86

Was it the proud full sail of his great verse,
Bound for the prize of all too precious you,
That did my ripe thoughts in my brain inhearse,
Making their tomb the womb wherein they grew?
Was it his spirit, by spirits taught to write,
Above a mortal pitch, that struck me dead?
No, neither he, nor his compeers by night
Giving him aid, my verse astonished.
He, nor that affable familiar ghost
Which nightly gulls him with intelligence,
As victors of my silence cannot boast;
I was not sick of any fear from thence:
But when your countenance fill'd up his line,
Then lacked I matter; that enfeebled mine.

87

Farewell – you're much too dear for me
To possess alone,
And likely you are most aware
Of the worth you own.
And as you have such merit,
It's plain for all to see
That you have every right to thus
Break your bonds with me.
For how can I hold on to you
Unless you choose to stay?
For I don't warrant such a gift
What e'er one cares to say.
And so my right for your sweet love
Reverts now back to you,
You didn't know your value when
Our precious love first grew.
Or else you were mistaken
About the worth in me,
And so I give your great gift back
And do it readily.
And now a better judgement
You can freely make,
And as for me it quickly seems
I'm suddenly awake.
I've had you as a lovely dream,
And that sweet dream did show
That in this sleep I was a king –
But it's not really so.

87

Farewell! thou art too dear for my possessing,
And like enough thou know'st thy estimate,
The charter of thy worth gives thee releasing;
My bonds in thee are all determinate.
For how do I hold thee but by thy granting?
And for that riches where is my deserving?
The cause of this fair gift in me is wanting,
And so my patent back again is swerving.
Thy self thou gav'st, thy own worth then not knowing,
Or me to whom thou gav'st it, else mistaking;
So thy great gift, upon misprision growing,
Comes home again, on better judgement making.
Thus have I had thee, as a dream doth flatter,
In sleep a king, but waking no such matter.

88

When you're disposed to talk me down,
Although it isn't right,
I'll take your side and I'll agree
And 'gainst myself I'll fight.
I'll say that you are virtuous,
And I will not deny
Your unfair accusations,
Even though you lie.
And as I'm best acquainted
With traits where I'm not strong,
On all my little weaknesses
And things that I do wrong –
Because of this I can thus tell
A convincing story,
That shows that finishing with me
Is only to your glory.
And from this I'll gain, for I
Will bend love thoughts on thee,
And injuring myself will then
Help you – and thus help me.
For such is the great love I bear,
When I give help to you,
I aid myself and give myself
Twice the advantage too.
And because it is to you
I totally belong,
To make things right for you I'll bear
Every kind of wrong.

88

When thou shalt be dispos'd to set me light,
And place my merit in the eye of scorn,
Upon thy side, against myself I'll fight,
And prove thee virtuous, though thou art forsworn.
With mine own weakness, being best acquainted,
Upon thy part I can set down a story
Of faults conceal'd, wherein I am attainted;
That thou in losing me shalt win much glory:
And I by this will be a gainer too;
For bending all my loving thoughts on thee,
The injuries that to myself I do,
Doing thee vantage, double-vantage me.
Such is my love, to thee I so belong,
That for thy right, myself will bear all wrong.

89

Say that you did forsake me
Because I was at fault,
And I'll agree to all you say,
I'll not request you halt.
Whatever you should speak of me,
I will not take offence,
Criticise me all you like,
I'll offer no defence.
Say that I'm lame and I will then
Quite readily agree,
Accuse me any way you like
And it won't trouble me.
You can't disgrace me half as much
As I myself might do,
When I'm aware of what you want,
I'll do it just for you.
I'll strangle our acquaintance,
Make sure that every day,
I keep quite clear from where you walk,
I'll hide myself away.
Our warm familiarity
Will be quite at an end,
And people won't remember
That once you were my friend.
I vow to be my own worst foe,
And choose that novel state,
Because I mustn't love someone
That your dear self does hate.

89

Say that thou didst forsake me for some fault,
And I will comment upon that offence:
Speak of my lameness, and I straight will halt,
Against thy reasons making no defence.
Thou canst not love disgrace me half so ill,
To set a form upon desired change,
As I'll myself disgrace; knowing thy will,
I will acquaintance strangle, and look strange;
Be absent from thy walks; and in my tongue
Thy sweet beloved name no more shall dwell,
Lest I, too much profane, should do it wrong,
And haply of our old acquaintance tell.
For thee, against my self I'll vow debate,
For I must ne'er love him whom thou dost hate.

90

So hate me if that's what you want,
But do it – do it now,
While the world combines to thus
Confound me – make me bow.
So join the spite of fortune,
It's what I beg of you,
Don't wait until a later time,
Just hit me when they do.
Don't let me think that I've escaped
From losing you – then see
You follow on from other woe
To say you're leaving me.
Do not, I plead, pile up my grief
And add to all my sorrow,
Don't turn a windy night into
A rainy wet tomorrow.
If you're intent on leaving me,
There will be no relief
In waiting for the pain to go
From all my other grief.
Just leave me first – go right away,
I'll take all of the pain,
For if you choose another way
There surely is no gain.
For other hurtful things I bear,
Which now seem like great woe,
Compared with losing you my love
Would really not seem so.

90

Then hate me when thou wilt; if ever, now;
Now, while the world is bent my deeds to cross,
Join with the spite of fortune, make me bow,
And do not drop in for an after-loss:
Ah! do not, when my heart hath 'scaped this sorrow,
Come in the rearward of a conquer'd woe;
Give not a windy night a rainy morrow,
To linger out a purpos'd overthrow.
If thou wilt leave me, do not leave me last,
When other petty griefs have done their spite,
But in the onset come: so shall I taste
At first the very worst of fortune's might;
And other strains of woe, which now seem woe,
Compar'd with loss of thee, will not seem so.

91

Some people love exalted rank,
The fact their very birth
Has given a position
They think confirms their worth.
Others feel that they possess
Unique ability,
A special skill that places them
Over all they see.
Some take their status from their wealth
Or because they're strong,
Or from the fancy clothes they wear
As they flounce through the throng.
Some love their hawks and hounds and some
Gain pleasure from their horses,
But me – I gain no pleasure from
These fickle, vain resources.
I get no happiness from these,
There's something way above
Social status, wealth and clothes,
And that is your dear love.
And having this is better than
All these other things.
I wouldn't change it for the world,
Not for the wealth of kings.
But I'm still wretched – for it's true,
One future day you may,
Fall out of love with me and then
Take all your love away.

91

Some glory in their birth, some in their skill,
Some in their wealth, some in their body's force,
Some in their garments though new-fangled ill;
Some in their hawks and hounds, some in their horse;
And every humour hath his adjunct pleasure.
Wherein it finds a joy above the rest:
But these particulars are not my measure,
All these I better in one general best.
Thy love is better than high birth to me,
Richer than wealth, prouder than garments' costs,
Of more delight than hawks and horses be;
And having thee, of all men's pride I boast:
Wretched in this alone, that thou mayst take
All this away, and me most wretched make.

92

But carry on and do your worst
And take yourself away,
For I will only live as long
As you decide to stay.
For I will only be alive
And living happily,
While you remain and give your love –
Whilst you are here with me.
My life depends on your sweet love,
And if you hurt me – fie,
I have no need to worry for
If you hurt me – I'll die.
You cannot make me vexed – concerned
About your fickle mind,
For if you took your love from me,
An instant death I'd find.
I wouldn't go on living
If you weren't closely by,
And so I'm happy thus to love
But happy too to die.
And so my situation's blessed,
Whichever way it goes,
I'm happy with the outcome,
Wherever the wind blows.
But nothing's ever perfect,
As life is always showing,
Suppose you were untrue to me
Without me ever knowing.

92

But do thy worst to steal thyself away,
For term of life thou art assured mine;
And life no longer than thy love will stay,
For it depends upon that love of thine.
Then need I not to fear the worst of wrongs,
When in the least of them my life hath end.
I see a better state to me belongs
Than that which on thy humour doth depend:
Thou canst not vex me with inconstant mind,
Since that my life on thy revolt doth lie.
O, what a happy title do I find,
Happy to have thy love, happy to die!
But what's so blessed-fair that fears no blot?
Thou mayst be false, and yet I know it not.

93

And so I really have no choice,
There's but one thing to do,
Live like a deceived husband
And just pretend you're true.
And so your face will seem the same,
As if you still love me,
Although your heart is somewhere else,
Acting deceitfully.
And as your eyes could never look
Hateful, strained or strange,
There is no chance I would detect
That there had been a change.
The mood of many people
Is shown within their eyes,
Furrowed brows and wrinkles
Give away their lies.
But when the heavens fashioned you,
They issued a decree,
That your sweet face would show but love,
Your thoughts we'd never see.
That only love upon your face
Would ever thus there dwell;
Your looks should only sweetness
Reveal and ever tell.
But how just like Eve's apple
Your beauty does thus grow,
For you're not quite as virtuous
As your sweet outward show.

93

So shall I live, supposing thou art true,
Like a deceived husband; so love's face
May still seem love to me, though alter'd new;
Thy looks with me, thy heart in other place:
For there can live no hatred in thine eye,
Therefore in that I cannot know thy change.
In many's looks, the false heart's history
Is writ in moods, and frowns, and wrinkles strange.
But heaven in thy creation did decree
That in thy face sweet love should ever dwell;
Whate'er thy thoughts, or thy heart's workings be,
Thy looks should nothing thence, but sweetness tell.
How like Eve's apple doth thy beauty grow,
If thy sweet virtue answer not thy show!

94

Those people who are beautiful
And have the power to hurt,
But resist temptation and
Never ever flirt:
Those who are attractive
But choose to stand alone,
Who turn so many heads but still
Seem like a block of stone:
Those who're hard to tempt and wear
Cold and moody faces,
These are the ones who rightly
Inherit heaven's graces.
They care for Nature's riches,
And see it as their duty
Not to spread themselves around,
And thereby waste their beauty.
The summer flower is very sweet
As summer days go by,
Though to itself it merely seems
That it will live and die.
But if that flower's infected,
Then quickly, with all speed,
That flower becomes inferior
To the lowest weed.
For sweet things will turn very sour
By their untrue deeds.
Rotting lilies smell much worse
Than base and common weeds.

94

They that have power to hurt, and will do none,
That do not do the thing they most do show,
Who, moving others, are themselves as stone,
Unmoved, cold, and to temptation slow;
They rightly do inherit heaven's graces,
And husband nature's riches from expense;
They are the lords and owners of their faces,
Others, but stewards of their excellence.
The summer's flower is to the summer sweet,
Though to itself, it only live and die,
But if that flower with base infection meet,
The basest weed outbraves his dignity:
For sweetest things turn sourest by their deeds;
Lilies that fester, smell far worse than weeds.

95

It really is regrettable,
It's truly such a shame,
That you let imperfections,
That ruin your good name,
Look so sweet and lovely,
As in you they repose;
It's like a canker growing
Within a fragrant rose.
Oh, how you cover up your sins,
What trickery you use,
You show a sweet exterior,
Your sinful ways to lose.
The tongue that tells the story
Of your lascivious days,
Somehow then turns its censure
Into a kind of praise.
And it seems, to thus be so,
And clearly understood,
That your name has the power to make
Bad actions just look good.
What a home your vices have –
Your beauty serves to hide
All the bad things that you do,
They're buried deep inside.
But take heed, dear heart of mine
Your beauty's not abused;
The hardest knife will lose its edge
If it is badly used.

95

How sweet and lovely dost thou make the shame
Which, like a canker in the fragrant rose,
Doth spot the beauty of thy budding name!
O, in what sweets dost thou thy sins enclose.
That tongue that tells the story of thy days,
Making lascivious comments on thy sport,
Cannot dispraise, but in a kind of praise;
Naming thy name, blesses an ill report.
O, what a mansion have those vices got
Which for their habitation chose out thee,
Where beauty's veil doth cover every blot
And all things turns to fair that eyes can see!
Take heed, dear heart, of this large privilege;
The hardest knife ill-us'd doth lose his edge.

96

Some say your fault is in your youth,
Some say it's nothing less,
Than that great weakness simply known
As lustful wantonness.
Some say your grace is bound up in
Your youth and gentle calm,
And how you turn your faults into
A sweet, disarming charm.
It's like the basest jewel upon
The finger of a queen,
Because of where it is – it's held
In great and high esteem.
And all those sins and errors
That you so boldly do,
Are viewed as noble qualities
Because they're done by you.
How many lambs could a stern wolf
Catch with a clever scam?
If he could make himself to look
Just like a little lamb.
How many unsuspecting folk
Could you thus lead astray?
If you amaze them with your charms
In your seductive way.
But don't do that – you're part of me,
And so all that you do,
Affects your reputation and
Means I'm affected too.

96

Some say thy fault is youth, some wantonness;
Some say thy grace is youth and gentle sport;
Both grace and faults are lov'd of more and less:
Thou mak'st faults graces that to thee resort.
As on the finger of a throned queen
The basest jewel will be well esteem'd,
So are those errors that in thee are seen
To truths translated, and for true things deem'd.
How many lambs might the stern wolf betray,
If like a lamb he could his looks translate!
How many gazers mightst thou lead away,
if thou wouldst use the strength of all thy state!
But do not so; I love thee in such sort,
As, thou being mine, mine is thy good report.

97

As I've been absent from you
It's seemed like winter's here,
For you're what brings the pleasure to
That freezing time of year.
And I have felt so very cold,
It's seemed dark everywhere,
Just like a dull December day
With all the trees laid bare.
And yet the time we've been apart
Has been in summertime,
And then in teeming autumn, when
Crops planted in spring's prime,
Burst forth with all their richness,
Around and far and wide,
Just like a widow giving birth
After her husband's died.
Yet this abundant issue
Of autumn, seems to be
Like many abject orphans,
Or so it seems to me.
For summer and his pleasures
All depend on you,
And with you so far away
The birds don't sing or coo.
And even if they choose to sing,
They do it with dull cheer,
Because the leaves look pale and they
Dread that the winter's near.

97

How like a winter hath my absence been
From thee, the pleasure of the fleeting year!
What freezings have I felt, what dark days seen!
What old December's bareness everywhere!
And yet this time removed was summer's time;
The teeming autumn, big with rich increase,
Bearing the wanton burden of the prime,
Like widow'd wombs after their lords' decease:
Yet this abundant issue seem'd to me
But hope of orphans, and unfather'd fruit;
For summer and his pleasures wait on thee,
And, thou away, the very birds are mute:
Or, if they sing, 'tis with so dull a cheer,
That leaves look pale, dreading the winter's near.

98

I have been apart from you
Throughout the lovely spring,
When April dressed so beautifully
Put youth in everything.
It brings the spirit of the young –
Even Saturn leapt with glee;
That heavy spirit of old age
Just laughed and heartily.
Yet not the singing of the birds,
Nor the flower's smell,
Could make me love the summer days –
Succumb to summer's spell.
Nor did I feel great wonder
When Nature did disclose
The white of lilies and the red
Of a lovely rose.
Yes they were sweet, but only
Pictures of delight,
Drawn to seem like you and yet
Poor copies to my sight.
Yet still it seemed like winter
On every single day,
It didn't seem like summer
With you so far away.
And with the fragrant flowers
I played – and everywhere,
As if with your reflection,
As if you were right there.

98

From you have I been absent in the spring,
When proud-pied April, dress'd in all his trim,
Hath put a spirit of youth in every thing,
That heavy Saturn laugh'd and leap'd with him.
Yet nor the lays of birds, nor the sweet smell
Of different flowers in odour and in hue,
Could make me any summer's story tell,
Or from their proud lap pluck them where they grew:
Nor did I wonder at the lily's white,
Nor praise the deep vermilion in the rose;
They were but sweet, but figures of delight,
Drawn after you, you pattern of all those.
Yet seem'd it winter still, and you away,
As with your shadow I with these did play.

99

The violet is a forward flower,
Arrogant and bold,
So this is how I chided it,
How my words did unfold.
'Sweet thief – wherever did you steal
Your sweet and lovely smell
If not from my beloved's breath,
If truth you were to tell?
And the purple colour that
You wear with such great pride,
Was fashioned from my dear love's blood,
With which yourself you've dyed.'
I blamed the lily for it stole
The whiteness from your hand,
And marjoram buds, they took your hair,
And lovely roses stand,
One blushing shame – another
White with its despair,
Because they stole your colours they
Stand with discomfort there.
Another rose, not red or white
Has annexed your breath,
But for this theft, a canker
Ate him – and caused his death.
I saw some other flowers and
As far as I could see,
Their sweetness and their colour,
They'd taken them from thee.

99

The forward violet thus did I chide:
Sweet thief, whence didst thou steal thy sweet that smells,
If not from my love's breath? The purple pride
Which on thy soft cheek for complexion dwells
In my love's veins thou hast too grossly dy'd.
The lily I condemned for thy hand,
And buds of marjoram had stol'n thy hair;
The roses fearfully on thorns did stand,
One blushing shame, another white despair;
A third, nor red nor white, had stol'n of both,
And to his robbery had annex'd thy breath;
But, for his theft, in pride of all his growth
A vengeful canker eat him up to death.
More flowers I noted, yet I none could see,
But sweet, or colour it had stol'n from thee.

100

Where have you gone, my inner Muse?
You've left it for too long,
To speak and help me write about
The one that makes you strong.
Do you spend inspiration
And all your unique might,
Upon another's worthless song,
To make their base song bright?
Return, forgetful Muse, return,
Help me to spend some time,
In writing gentle poetry
Which has a worthy rhyme.
Address these poems to my love,
Unto the very ear
That enjoys your skill with verse,
And holds it very dear.
And so get up my lazy Muse,
And then with every care,
Survey my love's sweet face and tell,
Are wrinkles present there?
If they are written on my love
Make everybody say,
That they despise and massively
Time's powers of decay.
And give my love fame faster than
Time can destroy his life,
Prevent him being cut down by
Time's scythe and crooked knife.

100

Where art thou Muse that thou forget'st so long,
To speak of that which gives thee all thy might?
Spend'st thou thy fury on some worthless song,
Darkening thy power to lend base subjects light?
Return forgetful Muse, and straight redeem,
In gentle numbers time so idly spent;
Sing to the ear that doth thy lays esteem
And gives thy pen both skill and argument.
Rise, resty Muse, my love's sweet face survey,
If Time have any wrinkle graven there;
If any, be a satire to decay,
And make time's spoils despised every where.
Give my love fame faster than Time wastes life,
So thou prevent'st his scythe and crooked knife.

101

Oh truant Muse, how will you make
Amends for your neglect
Towards my love – it isn't right,
It's not what I expect.
For he contains both beauty
And truth – and they rely
On him and Muse, your own good self
He too does dignify.
So answer Muse – perhaps you'll say
Truth has no need to be
Given colour, when fixed to
Beauty all can see.
And beauty doesn't have to be
Laid down and finely versed,
For its truth to be obvious,
Its truth to be dispersed.
But just because my love requires
No praise, well then will you
Stay silent for there is a task
That you should really do?
For you can make my love outlive
A gilded, golden tomb,
And thus be praised in years to come –
You can preserve his bloom.
So Muse, I beg you do your job,
And I will teach you how
To make my love in future time,
Look as he looks right now.

101

O truant Muse what shall be thy amends
For thy neglect of truth in beauty dy'd?
Both truth and beauty on my love depends;
So dost thou too, and therein dignified.
Make answer Muse: wilt thou not haply say,
'Truth needs no colour, with his colour fix'd;
Beauty no pencil, beauty's truth to lay;
But best is best, if never intermix'd'?
Because he needs no praise, wilt thou be dumb?
Excuse not silence so, for't lies in thee
To make him much outlive a gilded tomb
And to be prais'd of ages yet to be.
Then do thy office, Muse; I teach thee how
To make him seem long hence as he shows now.

102

My love is very strong although
It may seem weak, I guess,
It's not that I don't love you,
It's that I show it less.
When someone speaks of how he loves
And peppers it with sighs,
It seems he turns his love into
A kind of merchandise.
Our love was new in springtime,
That's when I wrote of you,
But stopped, like singing nightingales
When summer's not so new.
It's not that summer days are less
Pleasant than they were,
When nightingales sang mournfully,
Causing quite a stir.
It's just that many lovely birds
Give forth their singing now,
Their music can be heard and from
Every tree's grey bough.
And so the bird's sweet chorus
Loses some delight,
For they're not quite as magical
When common to our sight.
And so just like the nightingale,
I make my silence long,
Because I really wouldn't wish
To bore you with my song.

102

My love is strengthen'd, though more weak in seeming;
I love not less, though less the show appear;
That love is merchandis'd, whose rich esteeming,
The owner's tongue doth publish every where.
Our love was new, and then but in the spring,
When I was wont to greet it with my lays;
As Philomel in summer's front doth sing,
And stops her pipe in growth of riper days:
Not that the summer is less pleasant now
Than when her mournful hymns did hush the night,
But that wild music burthens every bough,
And sweets grown common lose their dear delight.
Therefore like her, I sometime hold my tongue:
Because I would not dull you with my song.

103

Alas, for as a poet
I'm really not so good,
Even though I'm blessed to have
A subject I'm sure would
Be much more worthy with my words
Obliterated – gone –
For you would have more value with
My praise not added on.
Don't blame me if I cannot write
A decent verse these days,
Look in the mirror, then you'll see
Why I can't write your praise.
For you'll see there before you
A captivating face,
That overwhelms my poet's skill,
And so brings me disgrace.
So wouldn't it be sinful,
In striving thus to tell
Good things about my subject if
I ruined what was well.
For all I write about is what
Everybody sees,
Your graces and your lovely gifts
And all your qualities.
Your mirror then will show much more
When you look into it,
Than anything that can be made
Within my verse to sit.

103

Alack! what poverty my Muse brings forth,
That having such a scope to show her pride,
The argument, all bare, is of more worth
Than when it hath my added praise beside!
O, blame me not, if I no more can write!
Look in your glass, and there appears a face
That over-goes my blunt invention quite,
Dulling my lines, and doing me disgrace.
Were it not sinful then, striving to mend,
To mar the subject that before was well?
For to no other pass my verses tend
Than of your graces and your gifts to tell;
And more, much more, than in my verse can sit,
Your own glass shows you when you look in it.

104

Fair friend, you never can be old,
For your great beauty lies
Within you in the way it was
When first I saw your eyes.
Since then three cold, grim winters have
Stripped leaves from summer thrice –
And three beauteous springs have turned
To autumn in a trice.
In the changing of the seasons
I've seen all this and more,
Three Aprils with their perfumes,
Hot burning Junes I saw.
It is this long since first we met –
You had a fresh, soft sheen,
And still you keep these attributes,
For you're still fresh and green.
Ah – but beauty steals away,
Just like a clock's slow hand,
It leaves and no-one sees it go –
And thus I understand
That your sweet beauty which it seems
Is standing very still,
Has motion and deceives my eyes,
For it moves on at will.
To people of the future time,
I think it should be said,
Before their birth, the loveliest
To ever live was dead.

104

To me, fair friend, you never can be old,
For as you were when first your eye I ey'd,
Such seems your beauty still. Three winters' cold,
Have from the forests shook three summers' pride,
Three beauteous springs to yellow autumn turn'd,
In process of the seasons have I seen,
Three April perfumes in three hot Junes burn'd,
Since first I saw you fresh, which yet are green.
Ah! yet doth beauty like a dial-hand,
Steal from his figure, and no pace perceiv'd;
So your sweet hue, which methinks still doth stand,
Hath motion, and mine eye may be deceiv'd:
For fear of which, hear this thou age unbred:
Ere you were born was beauty's summer dead.

105

Let no-one say the love I have
Is like idolatry,
That I treat my beloved like
An idol – this can't be.
So don't accuse me just because
All my songs and praise,
Are all about one person for
This is no passing phase.
My love is kind today and will
Be kind again tomorrow,
So excellent and wondrous that
I have no need to borrow
From other subjects – for my verse
Is all about the one
Who never changes – so my words
Are constant, when they're done.
My verse is thus consistent,
For what I always do
Is write about these things that are
Kind and fair and true.
Three themes for just one person,
Wherein these three themes live,
What wondrous scope for poetry
This subject does thus give.
Fairness, truth and kindness have
Been seen upon their own,
Till now they've never been contained
In just the one alone.

105

Let not my love be call'd idolatry,
Nor my beloved as an idol show,
Since all alike my songs and praises be
To one, of one, still such, and ever so.
Kind is my love to-day, to-morrow kind,
Still constant in a wondrous excellence;
Therefore my verse to constancy confin'd,
One thing expressing, leaves out difference.
'Fair, kind, and true,' is all my argument,
'Fair, kind, and true,' varying to other words;
And in this change is my invention spent,
Three themes in one, which wondrous scope affords.
Fair, kind, and true, have often liv'd alone,
Which three till now, never kept seat in one.

106

When I look in the chronicles
Of times of long ago,
I see descriptions of the folk
Who used to live and so,
I read of just how beautiful,
Way back in wasted times,
Some of these people were and how
They live on in old rhymes.
Verses that praise ladies,
And knights, who now are dead,
That talk about the beauty
Of hands, lips, eyes and head.
And so I quickly realise
That with their ancient pen
These poets wrote of charms like yours,
That people had back then.
These praises must be prophecies,
For they foretell of you,
They surely had this skill because
Your image they thus drew.
But poets who live in these times –
They clearly understand
About your beauty for they see
Your beauty at first hand.
And though we've eyes to wonder,
Here in these present days,
At all your grace – we lack the skill
To give it ample praise.

106

When in the chronicle of wasted time
I see descriptions of the fairest wights,
And beauty making beautiful old rime,
In praise of ladies dead and lovely knights,
Then, in the blazon of sweet beauty's best,
Of hand, of foot, of lip, of eye, of brow,
I see their antique pen would have express'd
Even such a beauty as you master now.
So all their praises are but prophecies
Of this our time, all you prefiguring;
And for they looked but with divining eyes,
They had not skill enough your worth to sing:
For we, which now behold these present days,
Have eyes to wonder, but lack tongues to praise.

107

Neither my most fearful thoughts
Nor those of the whole world,
Could stop me thinking of the things
That have now all unfurled.
I keep my love still close to me,
Who some were wont to say
Would spend much time unhappily
By being locked away.
The mortal moon has been eclipsed,
And fortune-tellers mock
The very things that they foretold –
That were once set in rock.
For things that seemed uncertain are
Now fixed like night and day,
And peace holds out an olive branch
And says it's here to stay.
And having reached this balmy time,
My love looks fresh and new,
And death itself defers to me,
It's all that it can do.
For I will live for evermore,
Within the future time,
While death insults dull, tongue-tied folk,
I'll live on in this rhyme.
This poem is your monument
And you – it will display,
When wicked tyrants fall and when
Those tombs of brass decay.

107

Not mine own fears, nor the prophetic soul
Of the wide world dreaming on things to come,
Can yet the lease of my true love control,
Supposed as forfeit to a confin'd doom.
The mortal moon hath her eclipse endur'd,
And the sad augurs mock their own presage;
Incertainties now crown themselves assur'd,
And peace proclaims olives of endless age.
Now with the drops of this most balmy time,
My love looks fresh, and Death to me subscribes,
Since, spite of him, I'll live in this poor rime,
While he insults o'er dull and speechless tribes:
And thou in this shalt find thy monument,
When tyrants' crests and tombs of brass are spent.

108

Whatever could I ever write
That I've not penned before?
To show you my true spirit – that
I couldn't love you more.
What fresh, new words could I construct
To tell just how I feel?
To speak of your great merit and
Your magical appeal.
There's nothing I can add sweet boy,
But just like prayers divine,
I keep repeating praise of you,
Thus to confirm you're mine:
And I am yours for evermore,
For it is just the same
As when I first wrote verse for you
And hallowed your fair name.
And this, the love, I feel ignores
The ravages of age,
Heeds not the wrinkles on your face
As time turns every page.
For I still see you as you were
When you were fresh and young,
That's how I write and speak of you
With loving pen and tongue.
I see you as I first saw you,
When my love was first bred,
Though time and outward looks now show,
Love's reason is now dead.

108

What's in the brain, that ink may character,
Which hath not figur'd to thee my true spirit?
What's new to speak, what now to register,
That may express my love, or thy dear merit?
Nothing, sweet boy; but yet, like prayers divine,
I must each day say o'er the very same;
Counting no old thing old, thou mine, I thine,
Even as when first I hallow'd thy fair name.
So that eternal love in love's fresh case,
Weighs not the dust and injury of age,
Nor gives to necessary wrinkles place,
But makes antiquity for aye his page;
Finding the first conceit of love there bred,
Where time and outward form would show it dead.

109

Oh never say that I was false
Deep within my heart,
And that my absence seems to say,
And readily impart,
That my true love was not so strong
As it was once before,
For it still lives within my breast
And will for evermore.
I can no more divide myself
From my great love for you,
Than I could split myself in half –
It's just as hard to do.
You are the home of my dear love,
And if I'd been away,
Just like a traveller returns,
I would come back to say,
My love for you remains the same –
It never will grow stale.
I couldn't leave someone like you,
For my love will prevail.
To leave for nothing of true worth
In exchange for thee,
Is something I can truly say
You'll never ever see.
For in this wide, great universe,
You can be really sure,
I care for only you my love,
I care for nothing more.

109

O, never say that I was false of heart,
Though absence seem'd my flame to qualify.
As easy might I from my self depart
As from my soul which in thy breast doth lie:
That is my home of love: if I have rang'd,
Like him that travels, I return again;
Just to the time, not with the time exchang'd,
So that myself bring water for my stain.
Never believe though in my nature reign'd,
All frailties that besiege all kinds of blood,
That it could so preposterously be stain'd,
To leave for nothing all thy sum of good;
For nothing this wide universe I call,
Save thou, my rose, in it thou art my all.

110

Alas, it's true, I have gone here,
Around and everywhere,
And made myself look like a fool,
To people over there.
I've let my thoughts go different ways,
Performed old wrongs I fear,
By using new acquaintances –
Sold cheaply what is dear.
And it is so, I've strangely looked
Upon love and its truth,
And with false heart I've acted thus,
To try to gain new youth.
And when I've been unfaithful,
I've proved you're way above
All other people in the world,
It's proved you're my best love.
And now all's done, I'm finished
In running all around,
It's you I love and so my feet
Are firmly on the ground.
I will not stray again my love –
Cavorting's at an end.
I'll no longer take new lovers
And upset you old friend.
So welcome me back to your arms
And to your loving breast,
For next to heaven, my sweet love,
You are the very best.

110

Alas! 'tis true, I have gone here and there,
And made my self a motley to the view,
Gor'd mine own thoughts, sold cheap what is most dear,
Made old offences of affections new;
Most true it is, that I have look'd on truth
Askance and strangely; but, by all above,
These blenches gave my heart another youth,
And worse essays prov'd thee my best of love.
Now all is done, save what shall have no end:
Mine appetite I never more will grind
On newer proof, to try an older friend,
A god in love, to whom I am confin'd.
Then give me welcome, next my heaven the best,
Even to thy pure and most most loving breast.

111

I know you chide my luck because
I earn my living so;
The fact that I'm an actor is
Not what you'd wish to know.
You think it breeds bad manners,
Affects my morals too,
I know it's not what you would want,
For it's a curse to you.
My name is brought down by my trade,
My nature is subdued;
Like a dyer's hand I'm stained –
I wish I were renewed
And could return to how I was:
Take pity now I've made
My life amongst the public in
The vulgar acting trade.
I wish I could take medicine
To help in my defection
From my acting life – for it
Would cure my strong infection.
However bitter is the cure,
I'll take it willingly,
I'll take a double penance if
It will thus rescue me.
So pity me, my dearest friend,
For then we'll likely see,
That your kind pity is enough
To bring a cure to me.

111

O, for my sake do you with Fortune chide,
The guilty goddess of my harmful deeds,
That did not better for my life provide
Than public means which public manners breeds.
Thence comes it that my name receives a brand,
And almost thence my nature is subdu'd
To what it works in, like the dyer's hand:
Pity me, then, and wish I were renew'd;
Whilst, like a willing patient, I will drink,
Potions of eisel 'gainst my strong infection;
No bitterness that I will bitter think,
Nor double penance, to correct correction.
Pity me then, dear friend, and I assure ye,
Even that your pity is enough to cure me.

112

Your love and pity make amends,
And are a help right now,
To overcome the vulgar words
All heaped upon my brow.
For what care I if others
Speak well of me or ill?
As long as you think good of me,
And say you always will.
To me, you are the very world,
And I must find a way
To learn my traits both good and bad
From everything you say.
And as I listen to your words
And diligently strive,
Nobody matters barring you,
And I to none alive.
You decide what's right or wrong,
I don't heed to the crowd,
I throw their voice into a hole
Then they don't sound so loud.
This stops their criticism,
And their flattery too,
The only thing I care about
In the world is you.
I do not care that everyone
Neglects and ignores me,
It matters not a jot, for dear
I only think of thee.

112

Your love and pity doth the impression fill,
Which vulgar scandal stamp'd upon my brow;
For what care I who calls me well or ill,
So you o'er-green my bad, my good allow?
You are my all-the-world, and I must strive
To know my shames and praises from your tongue;
None else to me, nor I to none alive,
That my steel'd sense or changes right or wrong.
In so profound abysm I throw all care
Of others' voices, that my adder's sense
To critic and to flatterer stopped are.
Mark how with my neglect I do dispense:
You are so strongly in my purpose bred,
That all the world besides methinks are dead.

113

Since I left you, I'm confused,
And now I surely find,
I'm so caught up within my thoughts
That I seem partly blind.
For when I look at everything,
I am in such a state,
I find my eyes don't take it in,
I just can't concentrate.
I don't absorb the birds that sing
Through the passing hours,
Or take in all the beauty
Of the lovely flowers.
I just don't latch upon these things
I see before my sight,
Not the sweetest creatures or
The day or deep, black night.
Not the mountains or the sea,
The crow or cooing dove,
For everything I see becomes
A vision of my love.
For my two eyes just cannot see
Anything but you,
Whichever way I look around –
It's all that I can do.
I'm so replete with you dear love,
Whatever I thus see,
Seems wrong and looks untrue and so
It just confuses me.

113

Since I left you, mine eye is in my mind;
And that which governs me to go about
Doth part his function and is partly blind,
Seems seeing, but effectually is out;
For it no form delivers to the heart
Of bird, of flower, or shape which it doth latch:
Of his quick objects hath the mind no part,
Nor his own vision holds what it doth catch;
For if it see the rud'st or gentlest sight,
The most sweet favour or deformed'st creature,
The mountain or the sea, the day or night:
The crow, or dove, it shapes them to your feature.
Incapable of more, replete with you,
My most true mind thus maketh mine untrue.

114

Has my head been turned because
Of your true love for me?
Am I just like a monarch who's
Plagued by great flattery?
Or is it that my eyes take in
Exactly what is true.
Have I been granted magic powers
Due to my love for you?
And this then turns foul monsters to
A sight from heaven above,
Into sweet angels that look like
Your own sweet self, my love.
And every vision that is bad
Is turned to goodness too,
But maybe I have been misled,
That my first thought was true.
It's flattery I'm seeing like
A king who fills his cup,
And when it's overflowing drinks
The flattery right up.
But my eyes know what they're seeing,
They know it very well,
They know what I would like to see
And so that's what they tell.
And as my eyes are poisoned,
They too are taken in,
They love these untrue visions too,
Thus that's where they begin.

114

Or whether doth my mind, being crown'd with you,
Drink up the monarch's plague, this flattery?
Or whether shall I say, mine eye saith true,
And that your love taught it this alchemy,
To make of monsters and things indigest
Such cherubins as your sweet self resemble,
Creating every bad a perfect best,
As fast as objects to his beams assemble?
O, 'tis the first, 'tis flattery in my seeing,
And my great mind most kingly drinks it up:
Mine eye well knows what with his gust is 'greeing,
And to his palate doth prepare the cup:
If it be poison'd, 'tis the lesser sin
That mine eye loves it and doth first begin.

115

Those loving words I wrote before
Were something of a lie,
I said I couldn't love you more,
Without you I would die.
But at the time I really thought
The flame of love I wore,
Could not burn any clearer
Or brighten any more.
I reckoned it was probable
The passing hand of time,
Would thus one day erode the love
That once had seemed sublime.
That many passing incidents –
All sorts of diverse things,
Could come between my love just as
Things change the will of kings.
This might divert the strongest mind
And put it to the test,
So fearing time, I should have said,
'It's now I love you best.'
For I was certain how I felt,
Sure of my love for you,
Although I had my doubts about
The future not in view.
Yet love – it is a baby,
Thus might I say it's so,
That though my love is fully formed
It still has room to grow.

115

Those lines that I before have writ do lie,
Even those that said I could not love you dearer:
Yet then my judgment knew no reason why
My most full flame should afterwards burn clearer.
But reckoning Time, whose million'd accidents
Creep in 'twixt vows, and change decrees of kings,
Tan sacred beauty, blunt the sharp'st intents,
Divert strong minds to the course of altering things;
Alas! why fearing of Time's tyranny,
Might I not then say, 'Now I love you best,'
When I was certain o'er incertainty,
Crowning the present, doubting of the rest?
Love is a babe, then might I not say so,
To give full growth to that which still doth grow?

116

Let not the marriage of two minds
In any way by me
Be disparaged – said that they
Should not exist or be.
And love is never love if it
Remotely changes – no,
Or if it disappears and when
It sees its lover go.
This isn't love – love's constant,
It looks on every storm,
And always stays unshaken –
Rock solid is the norm.
And love is too the brightest star
To every wandering boat,
Its true worth can't be measured but
Its height we still can quote.
Love is not in time's control,
Though time's sharp sickle's blade,
Destroys the brightest lips and cheeks
That Nature ever made.
Love alters not as hours and weeks
Tick by and pass away,
It lasts until the edge of doom,
Until that final day.
And if it could be proved I'm wrong,
Why then this would befall,
I'd say I never wrote a thing,
And no man loved at all.

116

Let me not to the marriage of true minds
Admit impediments. Love is not love
Which alters when it alteration finds,
Or bends with the remover to remove:
O, no! it is an ever-fixed mark,
That looks on tempests and is never shaken;
It is the star to every wandering bark,
Whose worth's unknown, although his height be taken.
Love's not Time's fool, though rosy lips and cheeks
Within his bending sickle's compass come;
Love alters not with his brief hours and weeks,
But bears it out even to the edge of doom.
If this be error and upon me prov'd,
I never writ, nor no man ever lov'd.

117

Accuse me thus – it's fair enough,
Say that I've not paid you
The great respect and thankfulness
That really is your due.
I've neglected to appreciate
And frequently to say,
How much I value your dear love
Though tied to it each day.
I've spent my time with people
I hardly knew – but see,
This time is rightly yours, and so
You should have been with me.
I've hoisted a great sail and let
The wind blow me away
As far from you as possible –
I sadly have to say.
Write all my stubborn wilfulness
And selfish errors down,
Gather them together and
'Twill surely make you frown,
But do not shoot great daggers
Towards me with your eyes,
And don't allow new anger
Within your breast to rise.
I only acted in this way,
My sweet beloved dove,
To test the very constancy
And virtue of your love.

117

Accuse me thus: that I have scanted all,
Wherein I should your great deserts repay,
Forgot upon your dearest love to call,
Whereto all bonds do tie me day by day;
That I have frequent been with unknown minds,
And given to time your own dear-purchas'd right;
That I have hoisted sail to all the winds
Which should transport me farthest from your sight.
Book both my wilfulness and errors down,
And on just proof surmise, accumulate;
Bring me within the level of your frown,
But shoot not at me in your waken'd hate;
Since my appeal says I did strive to prove
The constancy and virtue of your love.

118

Just as we make our appetites,
Keener, sharper too,
By eating certain foods that give
A healthy glow right through.
Or when we make ourselves feel sick
Then vomit – thus this way,
We ward off maladies and keep
Feared illnesses at bay.
And so because I was so full
Of your dear ways, my sweet,
Though never cloying – I sought out
Some bitter things to eat.
I resolved to spend my time
With other people so,
I wouldn't get thus sick of you,
Then wouldn't want to know.
So I applied a medicine
To ills that were not there,
And I grew used to acting
As if I didn't care.
I tried to bring a remedy
To something that was good,
And by applying something bad –
For I misunderstood.
But I learned from this and now think
That what I learned is true,
That drugs like this just poison for
I'm lovesick over you.

118

Like as, to make our appetites more keen,
With eager compounds we our palate urge;
As, to prevent our maladies unseen,
We sicken to shun sickness when we purge;
Even so, being full of your ne'er-cloying sweetness,
To bitter sauces did I frame my feeding;
And, sick of welfare, found a kind of meetness
To be diseas'd, ere that there was true needing.
Thus policy in love, to anticipate
The ills that were not, grew to faults assur'd,
And brought to medicine a healthful state
Which, rank of goodness, would by ill be cur'd;
But thence I learn and find the lesson true,
Drugs poison him that so fell sick of you.

119

But oh what potions have I drunk,
If truth I am to tell,
That I thought would be sweet but then
Turned out as foul as hell.
I turned my fears into great hopes,
My hopes into great fears,
Losing what I thought I'd win,
Thus ending all in tears.
What wretched errors did my heart
Commit as though possessed,
Right at the very moment when
It felt itself most blessed?
My eyes have bulged and ogled –
I was the poor receiver
Of the great distraction of
This maddening, hot fever.
What benefits does evil bring?
For things that seemed so ill –
Through evil can be much improved,
Made even better still.
For when a ruined love's rebuilt
It surely is quite true,
It grows much fairer than at first,
It's better built anew.
And so I go back to my love
Who makes my life content,
And through my evil deeds get back
Three times what I have spent.

119

What potions have I drunk of Siren tears,
Distill'd from limbecks foul as hell within,
Applying fears to hopes, and hopes to fears,
Still losing when I saw myself to win!
What wretched errors hath my heart committed,
Whilst it hath thought itself so blessed never!
How have mine eyes out of their spheres been fitted,
In the distraction of this madding fever!
O benefit of ill! now I find true
That better is, by evil still made better;
And ruin'd love, when it is built anew,
Grows fairer than at first, more strong, far greater.
So I return rebuk'd to my content,
And gain by ill thrice more than I have spent.

120

That you were once unkind to me
Is help to me right now,
Because the sorrow that I felt
Gives me good cause to bow.
For I feel guilty over
How I've hurt you – you see –
If you felt my unkindness
As I felt yours to me,
Why then you've been to hell and back
And I have truly been
Just like a tyrant – quite as bad
As any ever seen.
I never gave a thought when I
Was unkind every day,
To how I felt when you behaved
To me – the selfsame way.
I wish I had remembered
That former time of woe,
And thus recalled how very hard
Great sorrow hits and so,
I would have said I'm sorry,
As fast as you did too,
Administered the humble salve
To give relief to you.
And so with these offences now,
We can quite clearly see,
Mine to you is cancelled out,
Along with yours to me.

120

That you were once unkind befriends me now,
And for that sorrow, which I then did feel,
Needs must I under my transgression bow,
Unless my nerves were brass or hammer'd steel.
For if you were by my unkindness shaken,
As I by yours, you've pass'd a hell of time;
And I, a tyrant, have no leisure taken
To weigh how once I suffer'd in your crime.
O, that our night of woe might have remember'd
My deepest sense, how hard true sorrow hits,
And soon to you, as you to me, then tender'd
The humble salve, which wounded bosoms fits!
But that your trespass now becomes a fee;
Mine ransoms yours, and yours must ransom me.

121

It is much better to be vile
Than have folk think you're so,
And when you find yourself reproached
For being vile and know
That you are really not at all –
But you're denied the fun
Of doing what folk say is vile,
Which you deny and shun.
For why should others who're depraved
View my lascivious ways?
And smile about it knowingly
With looks that do appraise.
And why when they have frailties,
Weaker than mine, why should
They pry into my own – decide
What I think bad or good?
No – I am what I am and so
Those who hustle me
Only expose their own true self
And their depravity.
It could be that it's me that's straight,
And they're the ones who're bent,
You cannot judge my deeds – and by
The tainted thoughts they've sent,
Unless they're eager to maintain
That all men have a devil,
And they are bad – and bad right through –
And in that badness revel.

121

'Tis better to be vile than vile esteem'd,
When not to be receives reproach of being;
And the just pleasure lost, which is so deem'd
Not by our feeling, but by others' seeing:
For why should others' false adulterate eyes
Give salutation to my sportive blood?
Or on my frailties why are frailer spies,
Which in their wills count bad what I think good?
No, I am that I am, and they that level
At my abuses reckon up their own:
I may be straight though they themselves be bevel;
By their rank thoughts, my deeds must not be shown;
Unless this general evil they maintain,
All men are bad and in their badness reign.

122

Your memory will stay with me,
Lodged deep within my brain,
For longer than within the book
You gave me – 'twill remain
There in my mind, long after,
What's written down – you'll see
That it will outlive any date
Until eternity.
Or it will last as long at least
As my brain and heart,
Till they pass to oblivion
And give up that prized part
That keeps you there, so very dear –
My memory can hold
Much more than books with written words,
For it must thus be told,
That I don't need to write things down,
For how I feel's above
The need for any book because
My mind contains your love.
And so I was extremely bold,
I gave your book away,
Deciding to just trust my mind
To hold you close each day.
To keep a book here in my hand
To just remember thee,
Would imply forgetfulness
Does reside in me.

122

Thy gift, thy tables, are within my brain
Full character'd with lasting memory,
Which shall above that idle rank remain,
Beyond all date; even to eternity:
Or, at the least, so long as brain and heart
Have faculty by nature to subsist;
Till each to raz'd oblivion yield his part
Of thee, thy record never can be miss'd.
That poor retention could not so much hold,
Nor need I tallies thy dear love to score;
Therefore to give them from me was I bold,
To trust those tables that receive thee more:
To keep an adjunct to remember thee
Were to import forgetfulness in me.

123

No! Time you shall not ever boast
I've changed in any way,
That I'm not as I was before –
This I won't let you say.
The brand new pyramids we see,
New buildings that arise,
Although erected higher
And reaching to the skies,
Do not seem strange and novel;
They're replicas – no more
Of buildings from a former time
That we have seen before.
Our lives are very brief and so
We cherish what has been,
We think old things were made for us,
And yet it's all been seen
In times gone by – and so I say
Your records I defy,
The present, past and what we see,
Those records – they all lie.
For they're made more and then made less,
And they become just waste
By the passing of you – Time,
By your continual haste.
So I'll stay true unto myself
For every day and hour,
Despite your scythe with cutting edge
And your relentless power.

123

No, Time, thou shalt not boast that I do change:
Thy pyramids built up with newer might
To me are nothing novel, nothing strange;
They are but dressings of a former sight.
Our dates are brief, and therefore we admire
What thou dost foist upon us that is old;
And rather make them born to our desire
Than think that we before have heard them told.
Thy registers and thee I both defy,
Not wondering at the present nor the past,
For thy records and what we see doth lie,
Made more or less by thy continual haste.
This I do vow and this shall ever be;
I will be true despite thy scythe and thee.

124

If my dear love for you were made
By the hand of fate.
It could be Fortune's bastard,
In that unfathered state.
And thus my love could be destroyed
Or in the passing hours,
Just cast away, or valued
Like weeds or lovely flowers,
And subject to time's love or hate,
But no – my love was made
So it won't suffer accidents
For it is unafraid.
It is not helped by those in power,
And as we clearly see,
Not borne down by malcontents
Who fight authority.
My love is not afraid at all
Of politics and such,
Carried on by scheming folk,
Who connive too much.
My love stands boldly there alone
Resolute and wise,
Not affected when good things
Or bad things may arise.
To prove my point, I contrast
All those fools of time,
Who died repentant – even though
They'd lived a life of crime.

124

If my dear love were but the child of state,
It might for Fortune's bastard be unfather'd,
As subject to Time's love or to Time's hate,
Weeds among weeds, or flowers with flowers gather'd.
No, it was builded far from accident;
It suffers not in smiling pomp, nor falls
Under the blow of thralled discontent,
Whereto th' inviting time our fashion calls:
It fears not policy, that heretic,
Which works on leases of short-number'd hours,
But all alone stands hugely politic,
That it nor grows with heat, nor drowns with showers.
To this I witness call the fools of time,
Which die for goodness, who have lived for crime.

125

Would it give me much pleasure to
Carry the canopy,
Of a royal monarch for
The whole wide world to see?
Would it really mean so much,
With honour to appear
In a great procession with
True royalty so near?
Or would I think it of such worth
To be equipped to say,
I've built great monuments – because
They quickly waste away?
Have I not seen those folk who dwell
On how they look and all,
Who court the rich and powerful –
To see them quickly fall?
Such people who are pitiful
Sacrifice much treasure,
By seeking fickle goals instead
Of having simple pleasure.
No – let me give my heart to you,
A fair exchange we'll see:
Not second rate – a mutual gift,
Your own good self for me.
And so I say begone paid spy,
For when a truthful soul,
Is impeached – the likes of you
O'er them has no control.

125

Were't aught to me I bore the canopy,
With my extern the outward honouring,
Or laid great bases for eternity,
Which proves more short than waste or ruining?
Have I not seen dwellers on form and favour
Lose all and more by paying too much rent
For compound sweet; forgoing simple savour,
Pitiful thrivers, in their gazing spent?
No; let me be obsequious in thy heart,
And take thou my oblation, poor but free,
Which is not mix'd with seconds, knows no art,
But mutual render, only me for thee.
 Hence, thou suborned informer! a true soul
 When most impeach'd, stands least in thy control.

126

Oh my lovely, treasured boy,
You seem to have a power,
Over very time itself,
O'er the passing hour.
And I your lover, truthfully
Seem to wither while
You grow more beautiful with age,
And do it in fine style.
If Nature who's the mistress
O'er ruin – has a way
To pluck you back and keep you
Safe from all decay,
Why she must have a reason,
To use her unique skill,
To then hold back the passing time,
And its effects to kill.
Yet you should still fear Nature,
You're just to her a pleasure,
And she won't keep you always
As her special treasure.
One day she'll have to pay the price,
Her audit will be due.
One day she'll have a debt to pay,
And she'll pay it with you.

126

O thou, my lovely boy, who in thy power
Dost hold Time's fickle glass, his fickle hour;
Who hast by waning grown, and therein show'st
Thy lovers withering, as thy sweet self grow'st.
If Nature, sovereign mistress over wrack,
As thou goest onwards, still will pluck thee back,
She keeps thee to this purpose, that her skill
May time disgrace and wretched minutes kill.
Yet fear her, O thou minion of her pleasure!
She may detain, but not still keep, her treasure:
Her audit, though delay'd, answer'd must be,
And her quietus is to render thee.

127

In days of old, complexions
That were very dark,
Were not considered beautiful:
Fair skin – that hit the mark.
But now a dark complexion
Is considered best of all,
And fair complexions, in these days
Have taken quite a fall.
And every hand now has the power
To form a borrowed face,
Sweet beauty's not so special now,
For it is commonplace.
Cosmetics have the art to make
A plain face lovely, so –
Somebody with true beauty
Is very hard to know.
Therefore my lovely mistress's
Eyes are raven black,
And so are very fashionable,
But quietly attack
Those people not born beautiful,
Who paint themselves and thus
Improve their looks – but denigrate
Real beauty with this fuss.
Yet her black eyes appear to be
So mournful, with rapt woe,
That every tongue declares as one
True beauty should look so.

127

In the old age black was not counted fair,
Or if it were, it bore not beauty's name;
But now is black beauty's successive heir,
And beauty slander'd with a bastard shame:
For since each hand hath put on Nature's power,
Fairing the foul with art's false borrowed face,
Sweet beauty hath no name, no holy bower,
But is profan'd, if not lives in disgrace.
Therefore my mistress' eyes are raven black,
Her eyes so suited, and they mourners seem
At such who, not born fair, no beauty lack,
Sland'ring creation with a false esteem:
Yet so they mourn becoming of their woe,
That every tongue says beauty should look so.

128

How often when you choose to play
Fine music with such ease,
By running your sweet fingers
Across those wooden keys,
The music does confound my ear,
For I don't understand,
But listening, I envy
The keys that touch your hand.
They leap and kiss your fingers while
My poor, sad lips stand by.
Lips should be kissing – not those keys,
And so lips blush and sigh.
To be so tickled like those keys –
How my lips wish they could,
They'd gladly exchange places
And be transformed to wood.
And as your lovely fingers
Dance o'er those wooden chips,
They bless them so much more than they
Bless my warm, living lips.
The keys seem very happy,
And almost seem to say,
That touching your sweet fingers is
Sufficient when you play.
So let them have your fingers,
For these I will not miss,
But I request one treasured thing,
Give me your lips to kiss.

128

How oft when thou, my music, music play'st,
Upon that blessed wood whose motion sounds
With thy sweet fingers when thou gently sway'st
The wiry concord that mine ear confounds,
Do I envy those jacks that nimble leap,
To kiss the tender inward of thy hand,
Whilst my poor lips which should that harvest reap,
At the wood's boldness by thee blushing stand!
To be so tickled, they would change their state
And situation with those dancing chips,
O'er whom thy fingers walk with gentle gait,
Making dead wood more blest than living lips.
Since saucy jacks so happy are in this,
Give them thy fingers, me thy lips to kiss.

129

Carnal lust when exercised,
Many would thus claim,
Saps energy and once fulfilled
Brings on a bout of shame.
And when lust raises up its head,
It's true to one sure rule,
It can make people murderous,
Bloody, savage, cruel.
Full of blame, untrustworthy,
Extreme and very rude,
And once it's done, it is despised –
Thought of as being crude.
They go beyond all reason
To quickly hunt it down,
And once it's had, they instantly
Hate it with fearful frown.
They say it was laid in their way,
To make the taker mad,
But having had their wilful way
They see their lust as bad.
They're mad in its pursuit and then
In its possession too,
But once it's over, then they wish
They hadn't seen it through.
The world is most aware of this,
But none knows very well
How to avoid this heaven which
Then leads men onto hell.

129

The expense of spirit in a waste of shame
Is lust in action: and till action, lust
Is perjur'd, murderous, bloody, full of blame,
Savage, extreme, rude, cruel, not to trust;
Enjoy'd no sooner but despised straight;
Past reason hunted; and no sooner had,
Past reason hated, as a swallow'd bait,
On purpose laid to make the taker mad:
Mad in pursuit and in possession so;
Had, having, and in quest, to have extreme;
A bliss in proof,-- and prov'd, a very woe;
Before, a joy propos'd; behind a dream.
All this the world well knows; yet none knows well
To shun the heaven that leads men to this hell.

130

My lover's eyes aren't like the sun
As 'cross the sky it slips,
And coral is far redder
Than her red, ruby lips.
And if the driven snow is white,
Her breasts are greyish brown.
And too, if hairs be wires she has
Black wires upon her crown.
Though I've viewed roses, red and white,
These colours I've not seen
In her cheeks – they're never there,
And they have never been.
And more delight is often found
In perfume that you smell,
Than in my mistress's bad breath,
If truth I am to tell.
I love to hear her speak – yet know
That music's lovely sound
Is much more pleasing than the talk
I hear when she's around.
I grant, a goddess, I've not seen
Walking by on high,
My mistress merely treads the ground
As she goes walking by.
And yet, by heaven, my dear love
Is every bit as rare,
As women who false poets
Have lied about – called fair.

130

My mistress' eyes are nothing like the sun;
Coral is far more red, than her lips red:
If snow be white, why then her breasts are dun;
If hairs be wires, black wires grow on her head.
I have seen roses damask'd, red and white,
But no such roses see I in her cheeks;
And in some perfumes is there more delight
Than in the breath that from my mistress reeks.
I love to hear her speak, yet well I know
That music hath a far more pleasing sound:
I grant I never saw a goddess go,--
My mistress, when she walks, treads on the ground:
And yet by heaven, I think my love as rare,
As any she belied with false compare.

131

You are just as tyrannous
And totally unbowed,
As those women whose great beauty
Makes them both cruel and proud.
For you know only just too well,
To my dear doting heart,
You are the fairest, precious jewel,
And have been from the start.
Yet some in all good faith do say
That your poor face alone,
Lacks what it takes to make someone
With fervent love thus groan.
I wouldn't be so bold to say
That they have got it wrong,
But to myself I say they have –
They've been wrong all along.
And to be sure I've got it right,
And to prove the case,
I moan and groan a thousand times,
Just thinking of your face.
And all this ceaseless groaning –
One upon another,
Proves to me you're beautiful,
More than any other.
There's nothing black about you
Except the deeds you do,
It's why folk denigrate your looks,
When they all speak of you.

131

Thou art as tyrannous, so as thou art,
As those whose beauties proudly make them cruel;
For well thou know'st to my dear doting heart
Thou art the fairest and most precious jewel.
Yet, in good faith, some say that thee behold,
Thy face hath not the power to make love groan;
To say they err I dare not be so bold,
Although I swear it to myself alone.
And to be sure that is not false I swear,
A thousand groans, but thinking on thy face,
One on another's neck, do witness bear
Thy black is fairest in my judgment's place.
In nothing art thou black save in thy deeds,
And thence this slander, as I think, proceeds.

132

I love your eyes so very much,
Though with them you can see
Your heart torments me with disdain,
And so, they pity me.
And having put on black they seem
Like mourners in a train,
Who with their great compassion
Gaze upon my pain.
And truly, the clear morning sun
That grants the world a feast,
As in the grey and lovely sky
It rises in the east,
Or the shining star that glows
At evening – in the west,
Don't look as good as your two eyes;
To me they are the best.
And let it be that you allow
Your heart to mourn for me,
For mourning seems to suit you well.
It brings true grace to thee.
If you take pity on me then
With every part of you,
This would be a lovely thing,
For you, my love, to do.
And if you pity me, I'll swear
Beauty herself is black,
And everyone is ugly who
Does your complexion lack.

132

Thine eyes I love, and they, as pitying me,
Knowing thy heart torment me with disdain,
Have put on black and loving mourners be,
Looking with pretty ruth upon my pain.
And truly not the morning sun of heaven
Better becomes the grey cheeks of the east,
Nor that full star that ushers in the even,
Doth half that glory to the sober west,
As those two mourning eyes become thy face:
O, let it then as well beseem thy heart
To mourn for me since mourning doth thee grace,
And suit thy pity like in every part.
Then will I swear beauty herself is black,
And all they foul that thy complexion lack.

133

I curse the heart that makes my heart
Groan – and readily,
For that deep wound it gives my friend,
It also gives to me.
Why is it not enough for you
To torture me alone,
Without enslaving my sweet friend?
What cruelty you've shown.
You've taken me from out myself,
I'm my own man no more,
But my good friend, my second self
Is hardest hit – for sure.
And so by him and by you too,
And by myself as well,
I've been forsaken thrice threefold,
Confined as in a cell.
So keep my heart imprisoned,
But let my sad heart bail
My poor dear friend's beloved heart,
And get him out of jail.
Whoever keeps their eye on me,
I beg you that you send
My poor heart along to guard,
My dear and loyal friend.
And yet you'll still torment me,
Because I dwell in you.
And since my friend lives in my heart
You'll own him – and me too.

133

Beshrew that heart that makes my heart to groan
For that deep wound it gives my friend and me!
Is't not enough to torture me alone,
But slave to slavery my sweet'st friend must be?
Me from myself thy cruel eye hath taken,
And my next self thou harder hast engross'd:
Of him, myself, and thee I am forsaken;
A torment thrice three-fold thus to be cross'd:
Prison my heart in thy steel bosom's ward,
But then my friend's heart let my poor heart bail;
Whoe'er keeps me, let my heart be his guard;
Thou canst not then use rigour in my jail:
And yet thou wilt; for I, being pent in thee,
Perforce am thine, and all that is in me.

134

So now I understand he's yours
And I'm pledged to your will,
I'll sacrifice myself to you,
If you will just fulfil
My wish for my friend's swift return,
To bring comfort to me,
But you won't do it and my friend
Does not wish to be free.
For you are grasping – he is kind,
He's only bound to you
Because he tried to help me out,
That's all he tried to do.
And now it's like he signed a bond
And he is in a jam,
For he is under your control
As much as I now am.
And what you think your beauty grants,
You take it all – and then,
You put yourself around and seek
The company of men.
And so you thus ensnared my friend
Who got mixed up with you,
Just for my sake – I've lost a friend
Due to the things you do.
Oh yes, I've lost – you have us both,
You have him physically,
He gives you everything you want,
And still I am not free.

134

So, now I have confess'd that he is thine,
And I my self am mortgag'd to thy will,
Myself I'll forfeit, so that other mine
Thou wilt restore to be my comfort still:
But thou wilt not, nor he will not be free,
For thou art covetous, and he is kind;
He learn'd but surety-like to write for me,
Under that bond that him as fast doth bind.
The statute of thy beauty thou wilt take,
Thou usurer, that putt'st forth all to use,
And sue a friend came debtor for my sake;
So him I lose through my unkind abuse.
Him have I lost; thou hast both him and me:
He pays the whole, and yet am I not free.

135

Some women have their yearnings but
You have what you desire,
For you have Will – another too,
More Wills than you require.
I know that I'm demanding but
I can fulfil your needs,
So add another will to that
On which your lusting feeds.
Since your desires and lustful ways
Are large – demanding too,
Won't you just let me have my way,
To give my will to you?
For you appear to find the wills
Of others tempting – then,
Rejecting mine but saying yes
To lots of different men.
The sea is made of water,
But still receives the rain,
Adding water all the while,
Time and time again.
So though you've got a Will, you should,
As well, accept my will,
And this will make your appetite
Grow even larger still.
You should think of all your lovers
As just a single one,
And have me as a part of it,
When all is said and done.

135

Whoever hath her wish, thou hast thy 'Will,'
And 'Will' to boot, and 'Will' in over-plus;
More than enough am I that vex thee still,
To thy sweet will making addition thus.
Wilt thou, whose will is large and spacious,
Not once vouchsafe to hide my will in thine?
Shall will in others seem right gracious,
And in my will no fair acceptance shine?
The sea, all water, yet receives rain still,
And in abundance addeth to his store;
So thou, being rich in 'Will,' add to thy 'Will'
One will of mine, to make thy large will more.
Let no unkind 'No' fair beseechers kill;
Think all but one, and me in that one 'Will.'

136

If your sense of right and wrong
Bothers you when I
Draw near and try to have my way,
I say, give this a try.
Pretend I am your lover Will,
Though it is me instead,
Just tell your conscience it's that Will,
Who's welcome in your bed.
Out of kindness, just for me
Fulfil my dear request,
And fill your treasure with my will,
And with my will be blessed.
And fill it full of wills, dear love,
But let my will be one,
For someone with desires like yours,
Just one is viewed as none.
Let me number in your lovers,
And though you'll likely view,
My poor self as nothing –
Of no account to you –
Remember though I'm nothing,
That still I'll always be,
Although a nothing, thought of as
A something sweet to thee.
Just love my name and then as time
Passes – love it still,
And then you will just love me
Because my name is Will.

136

If thy soul check thee that I come so near,
Swear to thy blind soul that I was thy 'Will',
And will, thy soul knows, is admitted there;
Thus far for love, my love-suit, sweet, fulfil.
'Will', will fulfil the treasure of thy love,
Ay, fill it full with wills, and my will one.
In things of great receipt with ease we prove
Among a number one is reckon'd none:
Then in the number let me pass untold,
Though in thy store's account I one must be;
For nothing hold me, so it please thee hold
That nothing me, a something sweet to thee:
Make but my name thy love, and love that still,
And then thou lov'st me for my name is 'Will.'

137

Oh blind fool love, what do you do
To my wrong seeing eyes?
For you distort my sight and turn
Reality to lies.
And yet my eyes know beauty,
But when put to the test,
They see the worst of women but
They think they are the best.
My eyes have been corrupted
By my too biased sight,
Gazing at the one who sleeps
With different men each night.
Why have my eyes misled me?
To make me closely tied
To someone who is wrong for me
And to my heart has lied.
But why then should my heart believe
Her love would be unfurled
To only me – when I know well
She's there for all the world?
And why should my eyes lie to me?
They see all she does do,
But they put on a pleasant face,
Deny it could be true.
And so my eyes and heart have erred,
They've got it all quite wrong,
They've loved a woman who's untrue,
And have done all along.

137

Thou blind fool, Love, what dost thou to mine eyes,
That they behold, and see not what they see?
They know what beauty is, see where it lies,
Yet what the best is take the worst to be.
If eyes, corrupt by over-partial looks,
Be anchor'd in the bay where all men ride,
Why of eyes' falsehood hast thou forged hooks,
Whereto the judgment of my heart is tied?
Why should my heart think that a several plot,
Which my heart knows the wide world's common place?
Or mine eyes, seeing this, say this is not,
To put fair truth upon so foul a face?
In things right true my heart and eyes have err'd,
And to this false plague are they now transferr'd.

138

When my sweet love insists she's true,
With little groans and sighs,
I tell her I believe her though
I know full well she lies.
I do it so she thinks that I'm
A naïve, simple youth,
Who's unschooled in the world's false ways,
Just doesn't see the truth.
I pretend I'm taken in
By her sweet lying tongue,
And even though I'm past my best
I think she thinks me young.
And so we both suppress the truth,
For why am I not told
By her that she dissembles and
Why don't I say I'm old?
It is because it's best to love
Someone that you can trust,
And the old don't wish to speak
Of age – this is a must.
And so I sleep with her and she
Sleeps with me as well,
And one thing that we never do,
We never ever tell
Each other what we really think,
We flatter – she and me,
We lie about each others faults
And do it knowingly.

138

When my love swears that she is made of truth,
I do believe her though I know she lies,
That she might think me some untutor'd youth,
Unlearned in the world's false subtleties.
Thus vainly thinking that she thinks me young,
Although she knows my days are past the best,
Simply I credit her false-speaking tongue:
On both sides thus is simple truth suppressed:
But wherefore says she not she is unjust?
And wherefore say not I that I am old?
O, love's best habit is in seeming trust,
And age in love, loves not to have years told:
Therefore I lie with her, and she with me,
And in our faults by lies we flatter'd be.

139

Don't call on me to justify
The cruel things you have done,
The hurt you've laid upon my heart
By your idea of fun.
Don't flirt with others with your eyes,
Just tell me to my face
Of how you've been unfaithful for
I know it is the case.
Use the power o'er me you have,
And do it openly,
Don't play your artful, clever games,
Just play it straight with me.
Tell me that you've loved elsewhere,
But when you're in my sight
Don't look around at other men,
It hurts and it's not right.
Why wound me with your cunning when
You have control o'er me,
For I cannot defend myself
As surely you can see.
But then let me excuse my love,
Because I think she knows
Her stare has caused me anguish so
She turns it on my foes.
Yet don't do that – because in truth
I am now nearly slain,
So kill me outright with your looks
And free me from my pain.

139

O, call not me to justify the wrong
That thy unkindness lays upon my heart;
Wound me not with thine eye, but with thy tongue:
Use power with power, and slay me not by art,
Tell me thou lov'st elsewhere; but in my sight,
Dear heart, forbear to glance thine eye aside:
What need'st thou wound with cunning, when thy might
Is more than my o'erpress'd defence can bide?
Let me excuse thee: ah! my love well knows
Her pretty looks have been mine enemies;
And therefore from my face she turns my foes,
That they elsewhere might dart their injuries:
Yet do not so; but since I am near slain,
Kill me outright with looks, and rid my pain.

140

Be as wise as you are cruel,
Don't treat me with disdain,
Don't try my tongue-tied patience
Time and time again.
For if you do, my sorrow
Will force me then to say
How much pain you cause me when
You speak to me this way.
If I could teach you tactfulness,
You might then come to see
It's better to pretend that you
Are so in love with me.
Like testy sick men when their deaths
Are close – have doctors tell,
How they are fit and healthy,
In fact they're getting well.
For if I should despair, I know
I might go mad, you see,
And then there is a chance I might
Speak very ill of thee.
And as the world has grown so bad,
A slanderer may find
That lies are often quite believed
By some mad in their mind.
To stop folk telling lies 'bout you,
To stop me going mad,
Keep your eyes honest – even if
Your heart's untrue and bad.

140

Be wise as thou art cruel; do not press
My tongue-tied patience with too much disdain;
Lest sorrow lend me words, and words express
The manner of my pity-wanting pain.
If I might teach thee wit, better it were,
Though not to love, yet, love to tell me so;--
As testy sick men, when their deaths be near,
No news but health from their physicians know;--
For, if I should despair, I should grow mad,
And in my madness might speak ill of thee;
Now this ill-wresting world is grown so bad,
Mad slanderers by mad ears believed be.
That I may not be so, nor thou belied,
Bear thine eyes straight, though thy proud heart go wide.

141

In truth, I do not love you
With eyes – for I confess,
My eyes can see a thousand faults
That you, my dear, possess.
For it's my heart that loves you –
For my very eyes
On looking at you cannot help
To very soon despise.
And so my heart does dote on you,
But I'm afraid my ears,
Do not like your voice's tone –
And to add to these fears,
I have no wish to touch you and
No wish to be invited,
To a feast where you're the dish,
I wouldn't be delighted
By your taste or with your smell,
But having said all this,
My wits and my five senses can't
Stop my heart feeling bliss;
Or stop it from thus serving you,
I'm like a man possessed,
My proud heart is a slave to you,
Whilst leaving me distressed.
Despite the plague this woman brings,
I count myself one gain,
For though she makes me sin, it's true,
She too awards me pain.

141

In faith I do not love thee with mine eyes,
For they in thee a thousand errors note;
But 'tis my heart that loves what they despise,
Who, in despite of view, is pleased to dote.
Nor are mine ears with thy tongue's tune delighted;
Nor tender feeling, to base touches prone,
Nor taste, nor smell, desire to be invited
To any sensual feast with thee alone:
But my five wits nor my five senses can
Dissuade one foolish heart from serving thee,
Who leaves unsway'd the likeness of a man,
Thy proud heart's slave and vassal wretch to be:
Only my plague thus far I count my gain,
That she that makes me sin awards me pain.

142

Loving you, this is my sin –
Your virtue makes you hate
This sin of mine – although there is
Good reason for your state.
It's grounded in your sinful love,
For if you thus compare
Your own immoral ways with mine,
You'll see you've been unfair.
And even if I should deserve
To be reproved this way,
Then not from those red lips of yours,
For it is true to say
You've kissed as many lips as me,
False words of love you've said,
And you have ended up to be
In many a wrong bed.
So let me love you as you love
These men with whom you sleep;
And have some pity in your heart,
And then I too will keep
Some pity deep within for you –
For if you wish to be
Desired by other men, why then
You should too pity me,
Or find, from your example
Those you want at your side,
Will not want you – your great desires,
May well just be denied.

142

Love is my sin, and thy dear virtue hate,
Hate of my sin, grounded on sinful loving:
O, but with mine compare thou thine own state,
And thou shalt find it merits not reproving;
Or, if it do, not from those lips of thine,
That have profan'd their scarlet ornaments
And seal'd false bonds of love as oft as mine,
Robb'd others' beds' revenues of their rents.
Be it lawful I love thee, as thou lov'st those
Whom thine eyes woo as mine importune thee:
Root pity in thy heart, that, when it grows,
Thy pity may deserve to pitied be.
If thou dost seek to have what thou dost hide,
By self-example mayst thou be denied!

143

Just like a housewife who thus runs
To catch a feathered friend,
A chicken who has run away –
As it's become unpenned;
And as the housewife hurries off,
She sets her baby down,
But the little child's distressed,
Its face takes on a frown;
And then the infant chases Mum,
But she ignores her child,
For she's intent upon the fowl,
Yet still the child goes wild.
So mother chases and the child
Cries out in deep distress,
And still the baby is ignored,
It's an unholy mess.
It is the same with you and me,
You chase somebody who
Has made it very clear they have
No interest in you.
And like the baby I chase thee,
From very far behind,
But if you catch the one you want,
Turn round, kiss me, be kind.
Play the mothers part and cease
My crying – make me still,
And if you do, why then I'll pray
You get to have your Will.

143

Lo, as a careful housewife runs to catch
One of her feather'd creatures broke away,
Sets down her babe, and makes all swift dispatch
In pursuit of the thing she would have stay;
Whilst her neglected child holds her in chase,
Cries to catch her whose busy care is bent
To follow that which flies before her face,
Not prizing her poor infant's discontent;
So runn'st thou after that which flies from thee,
Whilst I thy babe chase thee afar behind;
But if thou catch thy hope, turn back to me,
And play the mother's part, kiss me, be kind;
So will I pray that thou mayst have thy 'Will,'
If thou turn back and my loud crying still.

144

I have two lovers – one comforts,
The other brings despair,
The better angel is a man
That I'd call true and fair.
The other is a woman –
Such evil does reside
Within her for she tempts away
Good angel from my side.
She really hopes she'll put me
Quickly into hell,
And make my saint a devil and
Put him in hell as well.
She woos his purity to turn
My saint from good to bad,
And there's no way that I can tell
What success she's had.
For since they're both away from me,
And friends with one another,
I'm guessing that my saint is in
The hell world of the other.
And yet I'll never know the truth,
I cannot know for sure,
And I must live within this state
At least for a bit more.
So I will have to just resolve
To live my life in doubt,
Until the day the bad angel
Throws my good one out.

144

Two loves I have of comfort and despair,
Which like two spirits do suggest me still:
The better angel is a man right fair,
The worser spirit a woman colour'd ill.
To win me soon to hell, my female evil,
Tempteth my better angel from my side,
And would corrupt my saint to be a devil,
Wooing his purity with her foul pride.
And whether that my angel be turn'd fiend,
Suspect I may, yet not directly tell;
But being both from me, both to each friend,
I guess one angel in another's hell:
Yet this shall I ne'er know, but live in doubt,
Till my bad angel fire my good one out.

145

Those lips that love's own hand did make
Breathed out the words 'I hate'.
They came from my beloved so
They put me in a state.
She spoke thus and to the one
Who loves her more than life;
Her words cut through me savagely,
They cut me like a knife.
But when she saw my woeful state,
I saw immediately
Kind mercy come into her heart
As she spoke then to me.
She chided that sweet tongue of hers
For speaking such dark doom,
For normally she spoke nice words,
Not words that dripped with gloom.
She changed the words 'I hate' and by
Altering the end,
And turned them from an enemy
Into a faithful friend.
She changed it round the way we see
Night's followed by the day,
And like a fiend from heaven,
To hell thus makes his way.
She took the hate out of 'I hate',
And made it sound brand new,
By adding then the two fine words,
She added just 'not you',

145

Those lips that Love's own hand did make,
Breathed forth the sound that said 'I hate',
To me that languish'd for her sake:
But when she saw my woeful state,
Straight in her heart did mercy come,
Chiding that tongue that ever sweet
Was us'd in giving gentle doom;
And taught it thus anew to greet;
'I hate' she alter'd with an end,
That followed it as gentle day,
Doth follow night, who like a fiend
From heaven to hell is flown away.
'I hate', from hate away she threw,
And sav'd my life, saying 'not you'.

146

My poor, poor soul – the centre
Of this sinful world,
Which sees myself in conflict,
Rebellion's unfurled.
For I deprive my inner self
And make life hard for me,
Whilst dressing up my body
In costly finery.
And so the question should be asked
When time is such a thief,
Why spend so much upon a life
When that life is so brief?
You spend all of your money
On your body when,
That body will be eaten
By worms – like other men.
So is this what you really want?
No – feed your soul and try
To let your body pine for food,
And this will by and by,
Gain heaven's time by selling
Worthless hours and for
The chance to feed your inner soul,
Whilst your outside stays poor.
And in this way you'll feed on death,
As death feeds on all men,
And once death is quite dead there'll be
No more dying then.

146

Poor soul, the centre of my sinful earth,
My sinful earth these rebel powers array,
Why dost thou pine within and suffer dearth,
Painting thy outward walls so costly gay?
Why so large cost, having so short a lease,
Dost thou upon thy fading mansion spend?
Shall worms, inheritors of this excess,
Eat up thy charge? Is this thy body's end?
Then soul, live thou upon thy servant's loss,
And let that pine to aggravate thy store;
Buy terms divine in selling hours of dross;
Within be fed, without be rich no more:
So shall thou feed on Death, that feeds on men,
And Death once dead, there's no more dying then.

147

My love is like a fever
That gives to me no ease,
It makes me long for – all the time,
What causes the disease.
It feeds upon whatever
Will preserve the ill,
To please and to accommodate
My desires and will.
My reason and my common sense,
Who're doctor to my love,
Are angry their prescription was
Just given a great shove.
But now that I am desperate,
I readily agree
With what the doctor said – desire
Is very bad for me.
So now that I'm past curing,
I'm mad and quite bereft,
Restless all the time – there is
Sadly no hope left.
My thoughts and everything I say
Are like a man possessed,
As if I were quite mad, I speak
Untruths, not well expressed.
For I have sworn that you are fair
And beautiful as well,
When you are dark as any night
And really black as hell.

147

My love is as a fever longing still,
For that which longer nurseth the disease;
Feeding on that which doth preserve the ill,
The uncertain sickly appetite to please.
My reason, the physician to my love,
Angry that his prescriptions are not kept,
Hath left me, and I desperate now approve
Desire is death, which physic did except.
Past cure I am, now reason is past care,
And frantic-mad with evermore unrest;
My thoughts and my discourse as madmen's are,
At random from the truth vainly express'd;
For I have sworn thee fair, and thought thee bright,
Who art as black as hell, as dark as night.

148

Oh what kind of eyes has love
Put into my head?
So that I can't see clearly – caused
My judgement to have fled.
Or if they do see properly,
All that's within my sight,
What's happened to my judgement
To put good sense to flight?
If she, that my eyes dote upon
Is loveliest to know,
Why does the world say it's not thus?
It really isn't so.
If she is not most beautiful,
It means eyes don't see true;
When somebody is deep in love
It's something they can't do.
How can a lover's eyes see truth
When the disaster rears –
Of eyes so clouded all the time,
By all consuming tears?
I'm not surprised I cannot see
Clearly what's in view,
For the sun itself sees naught
Till clouds disperse anew.
Oh cunning love – the tears I shed
Act to keep me blind,
For if my eyes saw properly,
My love's foul faults I'd find.

148

O me! what eyes hath Love put in my head,
Which have no correspondence with true sight;
Or, if they have, where is my judgment fled,
That censures falsely what they see aright?
If that be fair whereon my false eyes dote,
What means the world to say it is not so?
If it be not, then love doth well denote
Love's eye is not so true as all men's: no,
How can it? O, how can Love's eye be true,
That is so vexed with watching and with tears?
No marvel then, though I mistake my view;
The sun itself sees not, till heaven clears.
O cunning Love! with tears thou keep'st me blind,
Lest eyes well-seeing thy foul faults should find.

149

Oh cruel love how can you say
That I do not love you?
For I speak out against myself,
And do it for you too.
Do I not think about you when
I forget myself?
You tyrant, it's for you I place
Myself upon a shelf.
Who hates you that I call friend?
And those you frown upon,
Do I then fawn upon them? No,
A faithful face I don.
And if you scowl at me don't I
Condemn myself and groan?
And what proud traits do I possess
That give you cause to moan?
I'll gladly be your servant –
And it is also true,
Everything that's best in me
Worships the worst in you.
I am commanded by your eyes,
They lead a merry dance,
For they have power over me
With just a simple glance.
But carry on and hate me
For now I know your mind,
You love those people that can see –
Regrettably, I'm blind.

149

Canst thou, O cruel! say I love thee not,
When I against myself with thee partake?
Do I not think on thee, when I forgot
Am of myself, all tyrant, for thy sake?
Who hateth thee that I do call my friend,
On whom frown'st thou that I do fawn upon,
Nay, if thou lour'st on me, do I not spend
Revenge upon myself with present moan?
What merit do I in my self respect,
That is so proud thy service to despise,
When all my best doth worship thy defect,
Commanded by the motion of thine eyes?
But, love, hate on, for now I know thy mind;
Those that can see thou lov'st, and I am blind.

150

From what power does your power
Come with such great might?
That makes you look so wonderful
Within my troubled sight.
For though you are found wanting
In so many ways,
You make me query what I see –
Like saying lovely days
Are not graced with brightness,
Of course this isn't true.
Where did you get the knack to make
Dire things look good in you?
And where did you find that great skill
With which you have been blest,
To make bad things in you appear
Better than other's best?
Who taught you how to make me love
You dear – is it my fate?
When the more I hear of you,
The more I've cause to hate.
And though I love what others
Contemptuously abhor,
Do not look down upon my love –
I couldn't love you more.
If your unworthiness gave birth
To such great love in me,
Then I'm the most deserving one
To be beloved of thee.

150

O, from what power hast thou this powerful might,
With insufficiency my heart to sway?
To make me give the lie to my true sight,
And swear that brightness doth not grace the day?
Whence hast thou this becoming of things ill,
That in the very refuse of thy deeds
There is such strength and warrantise of skill,
That, in my mind, thy worst all best exceeds?
Who taught thee how to make me love thee more,
The more I hear and see just cause of hate?
O, though I love what others do abhor,
With others thou shouldst not abhor my state:
If thy unworthiness rais'd love in me,
More worthy I to be belov'd of thee.

151

Love is much too young to know
What conscience is – but then,
A conscience is born out of love,
So gentle cheater when
You criticise me sternly
For all that I do wrong,
Be aware, you might have had
The same faults all along.
When you betray me, I thus then
Betray the nobler me,
For my soul tells my body
It's free to have a spree,
To have its selfish way in love,
So what then does arise,
On hearing your sweet name – it points
To you as its great prize.
And I am proud that you are mine,
To serve you far and wide,
To stand and do what you require
Then fall down by your side.
Don't think I lack a conscience
Just because you see
It's taking me all o'er the place,
And playing games with me.
Because the one that I call 'love',
Who I love best of all,
Makes my love rise as then it makes
My love as quickly fall.

151

Love is too young to know what conscience is,
Yet who knows not conscience is born of love?
Then, gentle cheater, urge not my amiss,
Lest guilty of my faults thy sweet self prove:
For, thou betraying me, I do betray
My nobler part to my gross body's treason;
My soul doth tell my body that he may
Triumph in love; flesh stays no farther reason,
But rising at thy name doth point out thee,
As his triumphant prize. Proud of this pride,
He is contented thy poor drudge to be,
To stand in thy affairs, fall by thy side.
No want of conscience hold it that I call
Her 'love,' for whose dear love I rise and fall.

152

In loving you, I know full well
The thing I surely do
Is break a promise – but my dear,
You have broken two.
For you're unfaithful to your spouse,
Your marriage bed you've spurned,
And to your lover, faithless love
You've selfishly returned.
You said you'd hate your other half,
But this you didn't do,
But why do I take all this time
To lay this guilt on you?
You may have broken promises
But I broke twenty so
I am much worse than you and this
I think it's right you know.
For I have sworn deep oaths about
How very kind you are,
Oaths about your love, your truth,
About your constant star:
To make you seem much better,
My eyes I blinded – for
I made them swear they hadn't seen
Those things they really saw.
For I have sworn that you are fair,
And so I've made my eye,
Swear against what's really true,
To swear a foul, gross lie.

152

In loving thee thou know'st I am forsworn,
But thou art twice forsworn, to me love swearing;
In act thy bed-vow broke, and new faith torn,
In vowing new hate after new love bearing:
But why of two oaths' breach do I accuse thee,
When I break twenty? I am perjur'd most;
For all my vows are oaths but to misuse thee,
And all my honest faith in thee is lost:
For I have sworn deep oaths of thy deep kindness,
Oaths of thy love, thy truth, thy constancy;
And, to enlighten thee, gave eyes to blindness,
Or made them swear against the thing they see;
For I have sworn thee fair; more perjur'd I,
To swear against the truth so foul a lie!

153

Cupid laid his burning torch
Down on the ground one day;
He very quickly fell asleep –
Then coming by that way
Tripped a maid of fair Diana,
Who very quickly took,
Cupid's flaming torch and plunged
It straight into a brook.
This torch with its love-kindling fire
Turned that little spring,
Into a lively, heated bath
That could cure anything.
People came from all around
With ills that they endured,
And that little spring would then
Ensure that they were cured.
But then my mistress glanced across
At Cupid lying there;
It lit his torch – to test it,
He touched my heart with care.
I became so sick with love
For I had been thus fired,
That to cure the way I felt
The hot brook I desired.
The brook gave no assistance,
But what did by and by,
Was that which gave Cupid new fire,
My mistresses keen eye.

153

Cupid laid by his brand and fell asleep:
A maid of Dian's this advantage found,
And his love-kindling fire did quickly steep
In a cold valley-fountain of that ground;
Which borrow'd from this holy fire of Love,
A dateless lively heat, still to endure,
And grew a seething bath, which yet men prove
Against strange maladies a sovereign cure.
But at my mistress' eye Love's brand new-fired,
The boy for trial needs would touch my breast;
I, sick withal, the help of bath desired,
And thither hied, a sad distemper'd guest,
But found no cure, the bath for my help lies
Where Cupid got new fire; my mistress' eyes.

154

I saw the love-god Cupid
Before he fell asleep,
Lay down his love inflaming torch
That caused true hearts to leap.
Then as he slept, a group of nymphs
Who'd vowed that chaste they'd be,
Came by and spotted Cupid,
And very gingerly,
The fairest nymph picked up the torch –
That love-inducing fire
That warmed dear hearts – and in this way
The chief of hot desire
Was disarmed whilst sleeping,
By a virgin who
Quenched the torch within a well,
It warmed the well right through.
It turned into a heated bath
That set diseased men free,
When they stepped in, it proved it was
A healthy remedy.
But when I too stepped in the bath
To cure my love for her –
For my mistress who enslaves –
This is what did occur.
Love's fire, it may heat water
Within that little pool,
But one thing water doesn't do
Is true love – ever cool.

154

The little Love-god lying once asleep,
Laid by his side his heart-inflaming brand,
Whilst many nymphs that vow'd chaste life to keep
Came tripping by; but in her maiden hand
The fairest votary took up that fire
Which many legions of true hearts had warm'd;
And so the general of hot desire
Was, sleeping, by a virgin hand disarm'd.
This brand she quenched in a cool well by,
Which from Love's fire took heat perpetual,
Growing a bath and healthful remedy,
For men diseas'd; but I, my mistress' thrall,
Came there for cure and this by that I prove,
Love's fire heats water, water cools not love.

Also by Richard Cuddington

**SHAKESPEARE'S TRAGEDIES
IN EASY READING VERSE**

Richard Cuddington applies his Easy Reading Verse to Shakespeare's Tragedies. These are some of the Bard's most famous and compelling plays. Retold here in simple and engaging verse, the drama and excitement unfold with an urgency and momentum that captures the essence of the original plays.

Here the reader will meet Hamlet avenging his father's murder, Romeo risking all for his Juliet, Othello borne down with jealousy, Macbeth plotting to obtain Scotland's crown and many other colourful and doomed characters.

The sheer drama of some of Shakespeare's most memorable and highly acclaimed plays is captured here in fast moving, entertaining verse.

And when you know what each play is about you may well be encouraged to find out more about what makes these people tick by venturing into the original texts, having crept under the literary barrier and already found a way in by the back door.

SHAKESPEARE'S COMEDIES IN EASY READING VERSE

Richard Cuddington offers his readers a new approach to Shakespeare which acknowledges the Bard's stature as England's finest poet and playwright but lays aside the trappings of that greatness to reveal what made him popular with his contemporary audiences and what can still enchant us today – the stories.

Here in Easy Reading Verse the author retells the stories of Shakespeare's Comedies with clarity, humour and a modern directness. Readers will meet Shylock demanding his pound of flesh, Jack Falstaff pursuing his 'merry wives', Petruchio taming his Katherine and many other unforgettable characters who leap off the page with the immediacy of cartoon personalities.

The straightforward language with its bouncing, infectious rhythms and uncomplicated verse add pace and humour to each story as it rapidly unfolds. In this way the author makes Shakespeare less intimidating to potential readers, showing that England's greatest playwright can be fun and encouraging all who enjoy these verses to sample the rich pleasure of the original work.

SHAKESPEARE'S HISTORIES & ROMANCES IN EASY READING VERSE

Here in Richard Cuddington's Easy Reading Verse are Shakespeare's Histories and Romances which take the reader on two separate journeys. One through various turbulent periods of English history – the other through the slightly calmer waters of romance.

All the stories are told in clear and rhythmic verse which enhances the many dramatic and romantic situations. Readers will be entranced by the very diversity and richness of the colourful plots.

Here we meet Richard the Second losing his throne, Henry the Fifth conquering the French at Agincourt and Richard the Third using all his dastardly wiles to keep the crown. In contrast the Romances will introduce Prospero whipping up a tempest, Pericles losing, then finding his Thaisa and Palamon and Arcite fighting for the hand of Emilia. A veritable pageant of drama, turmoil and intrigue is encapsulated in these enthralling stories which are truly some of the Bard's finest plays.

These adaptations are an enjoyable and riveting read and act as an excellent bridge to the original texts.

CHAUCER'S CANTERBURY TALES IN EASY READING VERSE

For all its great reputation and the affection in which it is held, Chaucer's Canterbury Tales, written in 14th century Middle English, can actually be a daunting prospect to read. Richard Cuddington now steps in with a novel approach to Chaucer's famous gallery of pilgrims with their tales of chivalry, romance, courtly love, treachery, avarice, bawdiness, humour and nobility.

Whether you're new to the tales, or perhaps a teacher looking to enthuse and stimulate your students, or simply thinking of re-reading them, you will find here a thoroughly entertaining and immediately accessible way in to the storytelling genius of Chaucer in simple and amusing rhyming verse.

CHARLES DICKENS' OLIVER TWIST IN EASY READING VERSE

Oliver Twist has been a family favourite ever since Charles Dickens gave birth to his marvellous story in 1837. It has been reproduced in many ways but now Richard Cuddington applies his Easy Reading Verse to recount this famous tale.

Here are all the familiar cast of characters – brought to life in fun, uplifting narrative verse that moves along at a vibrant pace. From the moment of Oliver's birth in the Workhouse, through all his adventures at the hands of Fagin and Bill Sikes until he finally finds a new life – there is never a dull moment.

The author has previously applied his straightforward, rhythmic style to The Complete Works of Shakespeare and Chaucer's Canterbury Tales and now turns to Dickens' famous story to retell it in a way that will have great appeal to children and adults alike.

CHARLES DICKENS' A CHRISTMAS CAROL IN EASY READING VERSE

Charles Dickens' A Christmas Carol is arguably the most dearly loved Christmas story ever written – a favourite with the whole family. Whether you are one of the many fans of the story or possibly even new to the tale – you will surely enjoy this adaptation, written in fast moving, light-hearted verse. Author Richard Cuddington, who has already adapted the complete works of Shakespeare and Chaucer's Canterbury Tales into fun filled, narrative verse, now applies his rhythmic style to this famous classic. Here is Scrooge in all his miserly misery, slowly being converted from his former monstrous self into a being who really knows how to celebrate Christmas. The charming verse takes us on an unstoppable journey where we meet the Spirits of Christmas Past, Present and Future, the joyful Mr. Fezziwig and of course, the tragic but lovable figure of Tiny Tim. And on the way Scrooge dominates a tale that celebrates the joy of Christmas, encouraging a belief that we should embrace its spirit throughout the year.

KENNETH GRAHAME'S
THE WIND IN THE WILLOWS
IN EASY READING VERSE

Here is a delightful re-telling of one of Britain's best-loved books, aimed at younger children but also providing a treat for Grahame's established legion of fans of all ages. Richard Cuddington's verse rendition of Kenneth Grahame's The Wind in the Willows is the perfect introduction to a volume of stories which have enchanted generations of readers with its timeless evocation of life 'along the river bank'. All the well-known characters are here: the Mole, the Water Rat, Badger, Otter and, of course, the larger-than-life and utterly irrepressible Mr Toad of Toad Hall. The author has retained all the verve and energy of the original tales, but simplified the language to make them more accessible to the younger reader. Mole's frightening visit to the Wild Wood in the depths of winter and the colourful adventures of Toad take centre stage in bubbling rhythmic verse that drives the ebullient narrative forward so that there is never a dull moment.

www.ingramcontent.com/pod-product-compliance
Lightning Source LLC
Chambersburg PA
CBHW071219080526
44587CB00013BA/1430